NIGHT DRIVING

ALSO BY ADDIE ZIERMAN

When We Were on Fire

NIGHT DRIVING

A Story of Faith in the Dark

ADDIE ZIERMAN

CONVERGENT
BOOKS
NEW YORK

Published in the United States by Convergent Books, an imprint of the Crown
Publishing Group, a division of Penguin Random House LLC, New York.
www.crownpublishing.com

CONVERGENT BOOKS and its open book colophon are registered
trademarks of Penguin Random House LLC.

Library of Congress Cataloging-in-Publication Data
Names: Zierman, Addie, author.
Title: Night driving / Addie Zierman.
Description: First Edition. | New York : Convergent Books, 2016.
Identifiers: LCCN 2015039482 | ISBN 9781601425478 (pbk.) |
ISBN 9781601425485 (ebook)
Subjects: LCSH: Zierman, Addie. | Christian biography—United States.
Classification: LCC BR1725.Z54 A3 2016 | DDC 277.3/083092—dc23
LC record available at http://lccn.loc.gov/2015039482

ISBN 978-1-60142-547-8
eBook ISBN 978-1-60142-548-5

Printed in the United States of America

Book design by Lauren Dong
Cover design by Jenny Carrow
Cover photograph by Getty Images

10 9 8 7 6 5 4 3 2 1

First Edition

For my sons

Contents

PART IV

NIGHT DRIVING

Introduction to a Winter Road Trip

February 2014

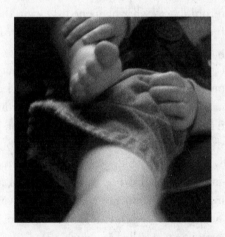

If you remember this trip at all, it will be in the blurred sounds of Disney DVDs against the rough highway. You'll remember it like the sun streaking orange through the windows of our minivan, sitting warm and heavy on your laps like a purring, striped tabby.

Maybe you'll remember fragments of these long days: the sun-bleached backs of dozens of baby alligators, piled on top of one another like lumber in that restaurant lagoon in Georgia. The seashells you lined up along a worn bath towel on a stranger's guest-bathroom sink. The rough beauty of those pinecones you gathered from that farm forest in North Carolina, hand in hand with a woman you will likely have forgotten by now.

Maybe you'll remember nothing, but you'll be tricked into *thinking* that you remember because of the pictures you'll see through the years, photographs turned into half-imagined memories in your still-solidifying minds: That shot of the two of you standing ankle-deep in the restless blue of the Atlantic. The one of you with the giant plastic roadside elephants. That hastily taken selfie of me, thirty years old, pantomiming a shout of enthusiasm as we entered *Florida*. The two of you asleep in your car seats behind me for the first time all day.

For the record, here's what happened: During the February of 2014, we left our home in Minnesota for no good reason at all and drove south. Dane, you were four. Liam, two.

You won't remember the few wiry gray hairs that began shooting out of my parted blond hair that winter, but I do: ten and a half years married, mama of two, running away from it all.

I stood in front of the streaked bathroom mirror, pulling at the grays, one sharp swift tug after another. Liam, you stood below me, carefully brushing my blue jeans with a Walmart hairbrush. In the face-magnifying mirror on the wall, I could see the crow's-feet sprawling outward from my eyes and that worry line fixed stubbornly between my eyebrows. (You called them "eye browns" then. My worry line you called an "ouchie.")

The woman standing in the halo of those halogen lights felt to me like a watermark, a ghost, some streaky, half-realized version of the person I imagined I'd be by now: Whole. Happy. One of those "fun moms," with a smile on her face and a spring in her step and lots of ideas for macaroni-based crafts. Instead I felt stripped bare as a tree branch—brittle and sharp and falling apart, still, after all this time.

Will you remember this? The mornings I stumbled out of bed only after you'd poked and tugged and hollered and I couldn't ignore you anymore? I lay on the couch in bleach-stained yoga pants and a ratty sweatshirt, hair piled sloppily at the nape of my neck, and I let one PBS kids' show bleed into another all day long.

I read . . . or didn't. Cleaned . . . or didn't. You wanted to play in the snow, but I couldn't manage to work myself up to it, so I lugged the bikes and riding toys into the house instead, and you rode them back and forth from the front door to the patio door, leaving salt streaks on the wood floors. You were slamming into things and leaving bits of drywall and paint in the corners and scars in the walls, whooping and laughing and unaware.

At night I fixed your dinner, then stood behind the counter and filled my wineglass to the brim with cheap cabernet. You ate your grapes and picked at your tacos and elbowed each other and whined about the vegetables. *Be kind to each other,* I told you. And you couldn't have known what was happening, really, when I drained the glass all the way to the bottom in a few smooth motions—and then filled it to the top again. You couldn't have guessed at the small, terrifying ways that I felt myself giving up.

After the third time school was closed in our district for freezing windchills, I began to trace a route from Minnesota to Florida on a map with my index finger. By then we'd had forty-seven days of below-zero temperatures in our suburban Minnesota town. The coldest winter in a generation, the weathermen were saying, and I believed them.

That week I created a new document titled "Epic Winter Road Trip?" where I calculated the time it would take us to get to Florida and listed the names of friends and family and acquaintances we might be able to crash with along the way. *Minnesota to Buffalo Grove, Illinois,* where my parents lived *(6 hours, 15 minutes). Buffalo Grove to Indy (3 hours, 15 minutes). Indy to Nashville (4 hours, 36 minutes).* And although the trip had been more of a vague hypothetical than anything until that point, seeing it laid out like that in sans serif—even with a question mark after it—was something of a decision in and of itself. Once I saw that it could, theoretically, be done, there was nothing to stop me from doing it.

I would load you up into our van and pull out of our driveway, and the three of us would merge into the throng of American Road Trippers working their way across the continental United States. We would go for all the usual reasons that people go—and for a few reasons that I didn't have the courage to admit, even to myself. Mostly those reasons had to do with the darkness that pressed down on my partly healed places, making my heart throb painfully, reminding me of the ways I had almost ruined everything about this time a half dozen years ago. The ways I still could.

Nashville to Atlanta (4 hours, 15 minutes). Atlanta to Florida (6 hours, 13 minutes). Once we got down there, nothing much mattered. I believed in that sparkling romance-movie way that Florida would heal us. After that, who cared? It was just a matter, then, of getting home again, and I imagined that it would be nice to head back up the southern East Coast, to see the Carolinas, to wander among the pastel beauty that I pictured to be *Savannah.*

"You're so *brave,*" the clerk at the Dollar Tree told me a week later when I explained what all the little toys and treats were for—emergency boredom busters for the car. I planned to wrap them up and pass them to the two of you along the way to keep you from killing each other. "Going all that way by yourself!" She shook her head, and loopy, Dollar Tree earrings jangled against her sallow, blush-dusted cheeks. "I got two that age, and I would *never* do that."

"Brave," the dental hygienist said a few days later. I'd chipped a front tooth trying to force a needle through sticky-backed Velcro with my teeth and had to be finagled into the dentist's schedule before we hit the road.

"What were you trying to make?" the hygienist had asked, peering over the top of her white mask into my broken smile. "Lap desks for my kids to use in the car. Probably should have just bought them off Amazon instead." I'd rolled my eyes at myself then, and she laughed, and I explained the road trip, and she'd said *brave*. It was all so amicably conversational that I could almost pretend that there wasn't something darkly obsessive about the way I was trying to force together disjointed pieces of fabric and vinyl and sticky-backed Velcro, trying to create something *perfect*.

"I remember ages two and four!" the dentist said over the sound of grinding enamel a few minutes later as he sanded down the pointy groove I'd made in the tooth. The metal of his grinding tool tasted sour—or maybe it was the acrid taste of my own front tooth. "There we go," he said, peering in for a closer look, and I couldn't see much of his face behind the green surgical mask and the glinting overhead lamp aimed at my mouth, but I think he was smiling when he added, "You're one brave lady!"

"Thanks!" I slurred at him through the gargling static of hose and spit sucker, not sure even as I accepted the approving awe whether *bravery* was the right word for any of it. My heart is not, in the end, cut from an adventurous, seafaring kind of cloth. I am, generally speaking, a homebody, content with very little adventure in my life. I chose this trip not because I am brave but because I was desperate.

The two of you were wild in forgiving innocence that winter. You jumped from the couches to the coffee table in your matching Spider-Man pajamas, your laughter bouncing off the vaulted walls of our living room like a dozen Ping-Pong balls. And the way out of the darkness has always, for me, started with telling the truth. It starts with saying where I am, what I need, and then moving resolutely toward the Light.

"We're going on a trip," I told you at bedtime, Dane, a few nights before we left. (Liam, you were already asleep in the room next door, your face covered lightly with your blue crocheted blanket. You were too young to understand. In your life, at age two, you were simply along for the ride.)

"We're going to stay at a lot of friends' houses, and it's going to take a long time, but at the end we'll be at the *beach*!" I smoothed your bath-softened hair as you lay on the bottom bunk of your bed, surrounded by stuffed animals, staring at me wide-eyed.

"The beach?"

"Yes," I said. "And we'll find lots of shells."

"Cool," you'd said, your speech already slurred with sleep, looking at me through those half-closed blue eyes. And how could I tell you *sixty hours in the car*? I didn't really understand it myself at that point, and *hours* and *minutes* weren't the ways you measured life in those days anyway.

I didn't tell you *three thousand miles*. I told you instead to fill up your backpacks with your favorite toys, to give your daddy a big hug and kiss, to say good-bye to the dog.

It didn't seem to me like I was tearing you out of the fabric of your daily life, though of course *I was*. But it was only *two weeks*. It was an *adventure,* and if anyone looked unsure as I packed up the last of the bags in the car, I didn't see it. I only saw the road stretching forward toward some blurry, pastel tableau of hope.

In the back of the minivan, I hung a mesh laundry bag and stacked a half dozen carefully labeled totes full of clothes. FOR CHICAGO. FOR INDY. FOR NASHVILLE. Next to them sat two cardboard boxes filled with copies of my first book to sell at readings that I'd scheduled haphazardly along the way. I had packed our swimming stuff in a blue vinyl IKEA bag, lined up your shoes underneath the seats, and hooked your coats over each of your armrests.

On the passenger seat, I piled snacks—Aldi-brand chips in sealed, individual bags, Sunbelt granola bars, Ninja Turtle fruit snacks, those fluorescent orange "cheese" crackers with the peanut butter sandwiched between them. Next to those there was the box of wrapped Dollar Store gifts and teetering stacks of library CDs and DVDs. I balanced the iHome on the dash, since our Craigslist-found Honda Odyssey wasn't pimped out enough to include an iPod adapter jack. There was dark chocolate in the compartment on the driver's-side door. The phone in one cup holder, the travel coffee mug in the other.

"Who's ready!" I shouted as we backed out of the driveway and toward the road. You didn't answer. You were too zoned in to the DVD players in front of your eyeballs, strapped into your seats, heading away from home for longer than you could have understood.

In the rearview mirror, a gray hair twanged like a spring from the winter static. And who knows if you'll remember any of this? The movies, the coats, the Dollar Store gifts passed back into your small, open hands.

My foot on the gas pedal, tearing toward the beach at seventy-eight miles per hour . . . because when you find yourself stuck in the cold, terrifying dark, sometimes the only way forward that you can see is to climb into that salt-streaked minivan and drive as fast as you can toward the light at the end of the ocean.

Part I

|||||||

*Whenever people talk to me about the weather,
I always feel quite certain that they mean
something else.*

—OSCAR WILDE,
THE IMPORTANCE OF BEING EARNEST

Andover, Minnesota, to
Buffalo Grove, Illinois

Wednesday, February 12, and
Thursday, February 13, 2014

"ROAD-TRIP SCENARIO," Andrew says. He's leaning against the kitchen counter on the night before the kids and I leave on our Epic Winter Road Trip. The table is piled with half-packed bags and stacks of books and assorted items that I want to be sure not to forget. Phone charger. Ibuprofen. The kids' pool floaties. So we'd eaten standing over the counter instead. The kids have abandoned their divided plastic plates to go play, and the plates sit there in front of us, streaked with sauce and crumbs and the partially eaten crusts of their frozen pizza. Andrew and

I are tearing at a loaf of Trader Joe's cheese bread and calling it dinner.

"You stop at a gas station and then, after driving fifteen minutes you realize . . . *Dane's not there!*"

"Shut up," I say with my mouth full of bread. "That's not going to happen."

"Mom!" Dane calls from the living room. "We don't say that word!"

Andrew raises his eyebrows and shakes his head at me. "Yeah, Mom. We don't say that word." And I kick him halfheartedly in the calf.

"You're right. We don't," I call over the partition between the kitchen and the living room. "Sorry." Then I turn back to Andrew and whisper, "I'm not going to *lose Dane.*"

"But you do. ROAD-TRIP SCENARIO. What're you gonna do?"

"I don't know. Panic. Drive back to the gas station. *Why are you messing with my mind?*"

"Wrong!" Andrew shouts gleefully. "He was hiding under all your tote bags! You should have stopped and searched the car first! You lose!"

I smack him with a book from the stack on the counter. "Jerk."

"Mom!" Dane says again.

"Sorry."

Andrew has been making fun of my tote bags ever since he came up to our bedroom last night to find me hastily unpacking one of them, surrounded by dozens of piles of clothes, staring bewildered at the mess in front of me. I'd been packing too long, and it had all started to run together—all those bags, all those clothes. I couldn't remember what I'd done and what I had left to do. *What was in the Nashville bag? Where did I put that one pair of jeans? Which bag did I put the purple dress in? Had I remembered diapers in the Indy tote bag for Liam? Would we need sweatshirts in Georgia?*

"Why don't you just put everything in one big suitcase?" he'd asked me as I dumped out a canvas Festival Foods bag that I'd labeled CHICAGO—BOYS and prepared to start over with it.

"Because," I'd said, separating the dumped clothes back into piles—one for Dane, one for Liam. I needed three outfits for each of them, plus an extra in case of an EMERGENCY. Plus twelve—might as well make it fifteen—diapers for Liam. "This way I don't have to haul *everything* in every time we stop. We'll have just what we need for that place."

"Looks like it's working . . . great."

He'd laughed and kissed the top of my head then, and I'd thrown a sandal at him in mock exasperation as he slipped behind the door and went back downstairs to watch the Winter Olympics on NBC. I could hear him laughing all the way down.

Now I look over at the kitchen table, lined with those tote bags. It's taken me something like four hours to get them packed, labeled, and hauled down here. I'm not about to admit it to my husband, but I'm only 60 to 65 percent sure that I have everything we need.

I look across the kitchen counter at him, shake my head. "I'm not a fan of your little SCENARIO game," I tell him, pulling off another chunk of bread.

"Sure you are," he says.

Liam trundles in then, swaggering like a cowboy, static-haired and pink-cheeked. "Milk!" he demands.

"How do you ask?" Andrew and I say at the same time.

"Please."

Andrew goes to get a sippy cup out of the cupboard, and I watch him. His hair is getting a little shaggy at the bottom, and he's wearing that worn blue thermal shirt that's got holes under the armpits. We are in the middle of our red-painted kitchen, in the middle of our tenth year of marriage, in the early-middle years of our lives.

The Big Life Decisions that filled our twenties have, more or less, been made. We bought the dog and the furniture and the house in the suburbs. We had our babies, and then we had our miscarriages, and that last stark image of an empty sac on the ultrasound screen seemed so personal, so final—a period at the end of the question that was *our family.*

We'd settled into our family of four then, sprawled into the empty bedrooms of our home, traded in my little red pickup truck for that Honda Odyssey minivan with automatic sliding doors. I sold the baby swing at a garage sale, and he took the crib apart, and we sent Dane to preschool.

After ten years of marriage, we have grown used to each other's body, the space we take up in the bed at night, the ways we curve into each other during sex. We have become a series of small intimacies: leaning against the kitchen counter, dinner not quite done on the stove, our conversation interrupted over and over by escalating quarrels from the living room.

We are in love; we are a dozen years away from the heady, crackling experience of *falling* in love. I shave the back of his neck when he gives himself a haircut over our bathroom sink; he jump-starts the van when I forget to turn off the lights and kill the battery. His face feels more familiar to me than my own as I look at him across the counter: that wide smile, those dimples and crow's-feet that have deepened into his face, the way his black glasses sit on the bridge of his nose. The way his eyes squint when he smiles, when he says "SCENARIO." The sound of his laugh when I roll my eyes.

"Oh, come on, Presh," he begs, calling me by our abbreviated version of *Precious*—a name that started as a sappy joke but has become, over the years, the sentimental shorthand of our love. He says it so often that every once in a while Dane and Liam call me Presh, too.

"Okay." I soften. "I'll play your dumb game."

"We don't say *dumb,* Mom!"

"SCENARIO: You're halfway to Chicago when all of a sudden you hear a little *yip-yip* coming from the back of the van."

"You wouldn't," I say flatly. Our small, black-and-white Havanese-Lhasa mix looks up from under my stool with big, innocent, cataract-blurred eyes. He's been sitting there all throughout dinner, waiting for me to drop something.

"Marty has decided to come with you! Your dog stowed away!" Andrew's voice takes on the familiar raspy quality of his laughter. "What do you do?"

"Kill you," I say. "Beg my parents to keep him for two weeks at their place until we swing back through Chicago."

"Aw, come on! You can't handle one more fuzzy, friendly passenger on your Epic Road Trip?"

I fill my glass of red wine a tiny bit more. "I can't even handle one more tote bag."

Andrew laughs big, and it echoes against the vaulted ceilings, into the living room where Curious George is blaring, where Dane is raking noisily through the Legos, where the small, regular routines of our family unfold every day.

I smile at him, and I feel a low-grade ache at the base of my stomach.

I don't really want to leave him for two weeks. But the truth is, I've already thought through every terrible turn the road trip could take, and not one of them scares me like the dark scenarios that lurk in the dull light of the Minnesota winter and the depths of my own heart.

I'm not running away from *him;* I'm just running away. I'm taking a temporary absence from the subzero temperatures and salt-smeared roads. The fact that I am a stay-at-home mom feels like a convenient escape hatch from my life. I can take my children *with me,* bring this circus on the road, and call it an Epic Road Trip. I can chalk it up to a memorable experience and a winter vacation, and the festive spontaneity of the whole enterprise could almost make me forget that I'm running away at all. Though, of course, I am. I'm running away from my quickly depleting stash of Trader Joe's wine and from the endless pitch-black mornings, buzzing with a loaded kind of silence, sending me reeling into the echoing caverns of my own heart. I'm running away, maybe, from myself. Making one last-ditch dash toward the light.

The first time I found myself feeling this way—so darkly cavernous, so terrifyingly numb—was seven years ago.

I was twenty-three—married three and a half years, working my first grown-up job—an entry-level position writing online help modules from a gray cubicle in an office park.

That year I'd gotten into a habit of waking up at five thirty, groping for my work clothes in the dark while Andrew slept, and then slipping out of the apartment before he woke, careful not to let the door slam on my way out. It was a 1.4-mile drive through the dark stillness of pre–rush hour to the coffeehouse where baristas greeted me by name. I was among the Regulars—most of them middle-aged businessmen who came to sit at highboy tables and read their newspapers. They'd nod and grunt when I walked by. "How ya doin'?" they'd ask, and I'd tap them amicably on the shoulder and chirp, "Fine, fine."

But when the Regulars went back to their papers, I slouched deep into the faux-leather chair at the back of the coffee shop and guzzled dark roast so fast that I burned my tongue raw. In my lap the black Thinline Bible lay as heavy and unresponsive as a slab of concrete, wrinkling my business casual. The journal I kept that year was road-trip themed, though I felt myself going nowhere. Even my pen felt like a stopped-up bottle of Elmer's glue as I tried to write, write, write my way back to the girl I remembered being.

The girl I *wanted* to be was the seventeen-year-old version of myself—slender and sweetly wide-eyed, with size-two jeans and a white-blond ponytail and that colorful beaded necklace that I'd made while working as a counselor at a Christian summer camp. I missed the easy way I used to smile, the easy faith that welled up in my heart each morning like a sunrise and propelled me to the empty high-school parking lot an hour before class each day for Prayer Group.

That girl made journals out of vintage books and filled one each month with long, sappy prayers. She was the product of the vibrant nineties' evangelical culture—of youth rallies and Christian rock and Christian teen-romance novels. Her theology bore a striking resemblance to a bad Hallmark TV movie. God was the hero, she was the heroine, and everything felt sparkly and enchanted.

She was, admittedly, a little naïve, a little performance-driven, a little *young*. But at least she *felt God*. At least she felt *something*.

At the coffee shop that year, I clung to the arms of my black faux-leather chair as though it were the helm of a ship, the steering room of my sinking spirituality, the only place where I had any shred of control over what was happening to me. I wrote and read, underlined verses, ran my tongue along the bumpy, tender place at the roof of my mouth where the coffee had scalded me. I filled out Beth Moore Bible-study workbooks and listened as wiry headphones pumped sermons into my ears. More than anything I wanted to tunnel backward through the foggy ether to that girl— the one who felt it all.

But winter eased into spring and then sank deep into a muggy Minnesota summer, and nothing seemed to happen. Eventually I gave up trying to find her.

Instead I began to spend dusky late afternoons on a barstool at Don Pablo's, half sprawled into my bowl-size margarita long after most of my group had left the company happy hour. The bald-headed bartender learned my name and started putting extra tequila into my margs, and I learned that if I couldn't feel God, at least I could feel *this*—the rushing wave of alcohol lifting me up, up, up . . . and over.

That summer I was disrupting poetry readings with loudly slurred accolades, garnering the reproachful glances of the Minneapolis literati. I was sending peals of metallic laughter through darkly lit bars, and anyone who knew me would have known that this tinny sound was not *happiness* but desperation.

Then again, no one there knew me. Not really. Men whom I'd never seen swiveled on their barstools, gave me the once-over, and I grew drunker still on the heady feeling of approval. If it wasn't going to be that exhilarating storybook romance with God that I'd been sold at age sixteen, then I'd settle for these small flirtations. I began to seek it out, to seek men out in car windows on the highway, in the hallways of the office, and from the faux-leather chair in the coffee shop, where I'd traded in the Bible for a novel—and then, eventually, for a brown-eyed graphic designer who looked at me like I was the moon.

In the end the frantic, churning darkness that propelled me through that long year had been about a lot of things. It had been about my own loneliness and about God's silence and about a faith that had cracked wide open to reveal so many gaps. And, as it turned out, it had also been about *clinical depression*—a term that I'd thought was reserved for those who'd experienced actual trauma in their lives but which was somehow assigned to me when I finally walked into a therapist's office several months later. The almost-affair I'd been having had detonated like a land mine, sending sharp curls of shrapnel into my marriage, and I walked into Dr. Martin's office that first day a little hungover, a little weepy, a little shattered.

It was a long time ago.

Sitting in the kitchen with Andrew now, I almost can't remember what it felt like to sit in the sunken center of that leather couch, surrounded on all sides by geometric-patterned throw pillows—the ones that Dr. Martin sometimes made me punch in our sessions—the tamped-down defeat and sadness muffled again and again as I beat the cushions flat. The clock ticked, and I stared at the concentric circles on the rug, and week by week I clawed my way out of that dark place until I felt sure I had somehow emerged.

❖

Back at the kitchen counter, I shake myself out of the memory and take another bite of bread. Andrew is looking at his iPhone, checking the weather or the Olympics scores or Facebook. Something makes him smile, and his eyes crinkle at the corners, and I can feel it all over again—the steel edge of that familiar emptiness like a blade at the base of my neck.

It's an unbearable kind of déjà vu, and it's been cutting through me for weeks, as cold and undeniable as the North Polar Vortex that has shifted southward over us, spreading like spilled oil over the continental United States. Like the wine that spills out of the half-empty bottle now as I top off my glass. Andrew laughs a little, and the bite of cheesy bread that I'm chewing catches in my throat. I swallow hard as I try to muster a smile. "What's funny?" I ask him.

"Oh, nothing. Stupid Facebook meme."

"DAD! We don't say 'stupid'!" Dane hollers.

Andrew laughs again and looks back down at his phone. I slide mine over to me to check my own Facebook app.

Lower temps here today than in Alaska! Minnesotans are bragging/complaining in my news feed, and my Chicago friends are hashtagging their weather-related posts #Chiberia. In Antarctica ice plains warm and the penguin population slowly and invisibly declines, but in the northeastern United States thousands of flights have just been canceled and the National Guard was deployed not that long ago to Atlanta, Georgia, where unexpected waves of ice and snow swept in and stranded students overnight on buses. From here it's hard to believe that *anything* could possibly be melting. And it seems as if all anyone is talking about is the weather.

It was just ten days ago, during the coldest part of this icy streak, that American actor Philip Seymour Hoffman died. He was an addict who'd been clean for a long time, a brilliant actor who had somehow managed to outrun his demons for a good many years. Until he couldn't. There he was, strung out on drugs, lying on the bathroom floor of his Manhattan apartment. *Gone.*

At JFK Airport, planes were sliding off runways on account of all the ice, and bloggers were talking ad nauseam about Hoffman and the slippery nature of addiction. My minivan was sliding along the ice-glazed highways of Minnesota, my eyes sliding toward the other cars, looking to catch the gaze of some guy—just briefly, just for a second—looking to feel the electric jolt of approval. The wine bottle on the kitchen counter glinted and blinked like a Las Vegas arrow. *You are here,* it said. *You have been here before.*

I couldn't stop picturing how it had gone the last time. The lies I'd told, the slow curve of the car over the white lines as I drove drunkenly to meet the Man Who Was Not My Husband. The way I'd stripped naked my heart, if not my body, before his appraising eyes.

What I mean is that I know how easy it is to do things you never imagined you were capable of doing. To become the hollowed-out person you never thought you could be.

Now Philip Seymour Hoffman is popping up in my news feed again. Headlines are asking if he was being tortured by the love of two women. Is this, they posit, what inevitably caused him to fall backward into his addictions? Or is it just because *these things happen*? You go off the rails of your own life without ever meaning to. It happens. It happens to all of us in different ways, at different times.

It happened to me once. And what's to stop it from happening now to this mother of two, sitting in the glowing center of her kitchen next to her husband? What's to stop me from disappearing quietly into the snow-bleached world of the suburbs?

This is the real reason for the road trip. I'm going because I'm afraid of what might happen if I stay.

❅

We set out on our road trip on a Thursday, as soon as Dane gets out of preschool. I'm almost late picking him up because I keep running back into the house to grab things: Sunglasses. Computer charger. Ice water in sippy cups. Plastic grocery bags for trash.

When I pull away from our house, it's rushed and unceremonious. Andrew and I kissed each other good-bye this morning before he left for work. He held me for a long time in our tote-bag-filled entryway, my face pressed into his neck as I willed myself not to cry. "Love you," he whispered.

"I love you, too."

We stayed there, swaying in the mess for another long moment—until Dane started screaming about pancakes and the dog started barking sharply and it was time to get back to the business of morning time. "It's going to be amazing," Andrew said, as he stood on the threshold of the garage door in his pressed black pants and pin-striped dress shirt. "You'll see."

I smiled weakly and waved at him. And then he was gone.

And now *I* am gone, driving out of Minneapolis, my foot pressed onto the gas pedal as I pull out of Andover, Minnesota, at the beginning of a wave of rush-hour traffic. "Who's ready for an adventure?" I ask in my most upbeat, cheeseball voice. "Dane? Liam?" But Dane and Liam are silent, absorbed in a movie and in those tooth-chipping lap desks that I'd rigged up out of fabric and cookie sheets and Velcro.

At the northeast seam of Minnesota and Wisconsin, the hills roll serene underneath their blanket of snow, in and out of trees. There are spots when the interstate loops high enough that the landscape seems to stack on top of itself, and the muted winter sunset makes the whole thing glow before it dips away, disappears.

I sigh and reach for the coffee that I'd brewed at home, still hot enough in the travel mug to burn. I drink it anyway, let it scald the tender inside of my mouth as I think about all the times

I've driven this stretch—the pulsing vein connecting my current home in Minnesota to my first home in Chicago.

I've been driving this route several times a year ever since I first came up here for college a dozen years ago, my small green Honda loaded down with thrift-shop sweaters and Target-brand dishes and burned CD mixes. How many times have I done the drive since then? Ninety? A hundred? More? I pass the semi-truck weigh station where a cop is waiting in the usual spot, and even though he's been there nearly every time I've passed it, I still feel my breath catch with a low-grade panic and my foot fly to the brake pedal when I see him perched there, watching.

At Eau Claire the traffic backs up just a little, and the sudden blinking of a hundred brake lights brings to mind the hour-long traffic jam that stopped up that very first trip to Minnesota like a corked bottle. I'd idled, back then, in the driver's seat of my lit-tle car, eighteen years old and sporting a brand-new, super-short, college-girl haircut. I was at the precipice of the Future. I was sweating through my T-shirt.

I can still remember the moment it became clear that no one would be moving anytime soon, and we all put our cars in park and opened up our doors. Semi drivers were getting out to lean against their rigs and smoke and talk on CB radios. My windows were down, exhaust pouring into the car, music pouring out. "Drops of Jupiter" by Train was in the Discman playing on repeat. It was my theme song that summer, the dusty voice of Pat Mona-han singing the same question over and over: "Tell me, did you fall from a shooting star? / One without a permanent scar?"

When traffic had started moving again, and I'd finally inched my way to the site of the snag, all that was left of the commotion was the shell of a camper, its walls and fixtures burned away in some random roadside tragedy, leaving only the blackened metal frame.

Had it been some kind of sign? I wonder that now as we slide past Eau Claire. The last strains of sun are disappearing, and the blue night is yawning wide, swallowing us up. I didn't understand back then that you can't just drive away from who you are and start over—*blank slate*—somewhere new. It's more consuming than all that—the journey toward whoever it is you're going to become is always smudged with ashen remains.

The image of that burned-out camper stays with me as I'm carried farther and farther away from home. As I'm pulled along the cresting breast of the Wisconsin highway—south.

We drive, drive, drive. We stop, briefly, for cheeseburgers at dinnertime—and then drive some more. The movie screens mounted on the backs of the front seats shoot flickering rays of light across the car as the gray-tailed rat hero of *Ratatouille* finds a way to realize his dream of being a chef. I sip at my fresh cup of McDonald's coffee and keep glancing in the rearview mirror as the boys' eyes begin to close and their heads begin to droop heavily to the side. Somewhere in that blank, wooded stretch between Tomah and the Wisconsin Dells, they pass out. They fall asleep in quick succession—Liam, then Dane—like dominoes toppling.

Around us the infinite branches of the bare trees stretch and intertwine. The moon is round and heavy in the sky—technically *full* tonight at 98 percent visibility—and it's turning the whole sky the electric-blue color of a blank television screen. The darkness is backlit by some kind of light that I don't understand. The ultramarine brightness of it settles over the quiet heart of Wisconsin, highlighting it all—trees, snow, signs.

Silence. Solitude.

It's not new—this silence. Whatever small pipeline links me to my faith, to my felt experience of God, seems to have clogged up again . . . for no reason that I can pinpoint. Each morning for the last few months, I've rolled out of bed and padded down to sit in a hard-backed kitchen chair with the Bible open on my lap. But I haven't been able to read it. Instead I've been staring into the pitch-black morning as if I might find something there if I look hard enough.

But of course I never do.

Now I watch the trees thin around me as we approach the Wisconsin Dells, and it takes a near-herculean effort for me to offer a small prayer to the God of winter-striped fields, of reaching branches, of billboards and those who hang them. To the God of lonely highway crosses and adult superstores and gashed white lines in asphalt. Of roads taken. Of roads not taken. *"Find us,"* I whisper. *"Find me."*

Ahead I can see nothing but the indifferent blinking of red lights on a few faraway cell-phone towers. I look in the rearview mirror at my sons. Their blond heads hang at impossible angles against the sides of their car seats, the flickering pixels of their movie highlighting their features. There's still a smudge of ketchup from dinner on Liam's right cheek, just above his dimple. At some point he stripped off both shoes and socks. His blue jeans have bunched to reveal plump, pale ankles and bare, two-year-old toes.

Next to him Dane looks so big. This year the last of his rolling baby fat stretched out and disappeared into the angular arms and scraped-up legs of a bona fide *kid*. In the fall he'll start kindergarten, and I'm struck by the impossibility of time—the tall, pink-cheeked boy asleep in my mirror with his mouth half open, the paradox of slowly speeding years disappearing beneath us.

What will they remember about this? I wonder. What will they remember about *me*—the fragile, fractured mother of their earliest days?

The tree line splits open, and the Wisconsin Dells loom ahead of us—that strange, broken-down carnival of a town. Gas-station billboards promise diesel, cheese, liquor, and bait. Hotel billboards promise family togetherness and breakneck-speed water slides. This time of year, the Dells are both full and empty all at once. The lavish indoor-water-park hotels are stuffed with pale midwestern families, fleeing their winter lives for a mini-vacation, while downtown the storefronts look all but abandoned, fluorescent bikinis shivering in the windows, fudge shops frosted over with ice.

The kids shift in their seats as light streams in the window, and I hold my breath until they settle into sleep again. Then I reach back carefully to flip the DVD player off. Through the windshield, signs flash by: EXIT 87, EXIT 89, EXIT 92. The roads they mark are as familiar to me as the lines on my own face.

The fall and winter after my life went off the rails, I spent a lot of time in the off-season Wisconsin Dells. It was the natural (if somewhat abnormal) meeting place between my home in Minnesota and Chicago, where my two best friends, Kim and Alissa, lived at the time. This is what I'm thinking of now, as I drive my sleeping kids through the glowing heart of Wisconsin in the middle of this blue winter night. Those girls. Those immortal weekends. The small, important ways we are saved.

Outside the windows familiar landmarks pop up: The Polynesian. The Days Inn. The Kalahari, with its giant indoor Ferris wheel and its "adult nightclub" where we once sipped overpriced rum and Cokes and danced like mad to "Apple Bottom Jeans." To my right, that Walmart Supercenter where I got an ill-advised haircut while Kim looked down at her Jimmy Choos in embarrassed disbelief. The Desert Star Cinema, where we dangled our feet over the seats in front of us, drank wine from miniature bottles, and watched *Forgetting Sarah Marshall* as we tried to make sense of our own damaging and damaged relationships.

Tucked back around that curved place off of Exit 89, just beyond my sight line, is the Pizza Pub with its sloped red roof and its dim barroom off to the side of the family-friendly restart: A DELLS TRADITION SINCE 1983! How many nights did we sit at that highboy table by the bar, surrounded by the smoky exhalations of flannel-wearing locals, asking each other questions about God? There, next to our salt-rimmed margarita glasses and thick slices of pan pizza, we laid out our broken pieces and rearranged them until our fingers were bloody with the pain of it all and our faces were slack-jawed with tequila. And then we went dancing.

I sigh and dial Andrew on the phone, but it goes straight to voice mail. "Hey, Presh. Kids are asleep, and I'm halfway to Chicago." In the rearview mirror, the Wisconsin Dells become pinpricks of spinning light . . . then nothing. "Miss you already," I say, and I do.

On a Thursday night in February, there are few cars on the interstate, and I take a sip of now-cold coffee from my mostly empty McDonald's cup while we slip through the darkness.

ROAD-TRIP SCENARIO: You are driving through a blue Wisconsin night. The moon is low, and the kids are behind you, asleep. You're two hundred fifty miles into a three-thousand-mile road trip. *What are you even doing? What is it that you think you're going to find, anyway?*

A sign flashes by: CHICAGO—180 MILES.

I already have the cruise control set at seventy-eight—eight miles over the speed limit—but I bump it up a couple of notches anyway, and the van hurtles south.

We can get to my parents' house in two and a half hours if we don't make any stops.

Chicago, Illinois

Friday, February 14, 2014

On the platform of the Lake Cook Road Metra station the next morning, the wind is an ax sharpening itself against my frozen face while I wait for the train to Chicago. Around me, commuters stand in dedicated silence, staring ahead at the same invisible point on the horizon or peering into their phones, earbud wires snaking up underneath their hats into their ears.

From the corner of my eye, I stare at the strangers, cataloging their fashion and the things they carry: Briefcases and tailored, expensive-looking jackets. Coach purses and paper Whole Foods bags with handles. They seem to be an entirely different kind of people from the ones who inhabit my suburban world of SUVs and big, sprawling Target parking lots. My morning routine back home consists of tossing loose boots and jackets into the front seat of the heated minivan, the radio blaring loud, Liam screaming louder as I scramble to get Dane to preschool on time. But here on the platform of the Lake Cook Metra, nothing seems frantic to me. There is only an air of graceful detachment, a buttoned-up kind of sophistication that fills me with a sense of displacement. I can't stop noticing them: the commuting regulars who stand tall and nonchalant, looking the wind straight in its wild eyes.

I shift carefully, trying not to be too obvious about the fact that I'm struggling with the weight of the duffel bag that I'd labeled CHICAGO—ADDIE and my overstuffed green canvas purse. The kids woke me up at six this morning—confused and blinking in the change of scenery, then, all at once, thrilled to find themselves at Grandma and Papi's house in the Chicago suburbs. I'd lounged for a long time in my dad's leather easy chair in the living room, watching Dane and Liam line up Grandma's collection of toy animals on the maroon rug, before my mom looked at the clock and said, "You'd better get going if you're going to make it to the city." All of a sudden, it was much later than I thought. I'd showered hastily, done a slipshod job with my makeup, and guzzled Folgers out of a travel mug between bites of a granola bar on the way to the station.

The plan for this weekend is to leave Dane and Liam with my mom and dad for two days while I head downtown to spend some time with one of my high-school best friends—Alissa—until my book reading tomorrow night at a small independent bookstore in Lincoln Park. Someone sent me a picture this morning of the orange sign in the shop's window display. It's nestled between literary book covers and twinkle lights and says in artsy black hand lettering, JOIN US AS ADDIE ZIERMAN SHARES HER BOOK *WHEN WE WERE ON FIRE: A MEMOIR OF CONSUMING FAITH, TANGLED LOVE, AND STARTING OVER.* SAT, FEB 15, 7 PM. I'm new enough to this author-reading thing that I find it all charming and exciting. I hope I get to keep the sign.

It's the first—and most glamorous—of a series of readings and meet-ups I've planned along the route of our trip. The logic of the road trip itself still feels a little flimsy, and these events in support of my still-new memoir add a kind of legitimacy to the whole enterprise. They allow me to spin the narrative in my mind, just a bit. Not some desperate clichéd story: WINTER-CRAZED MOM RUNS AWAY SOUTH! But rather: QUIRKY MIDWESTERN WRITER DRIVES CROSS-COUNTRY WITH BOOK AND KIDS! It's a story I can sell to my readers and to my parents and to my mom friends. It's a story I can sell to myself.

I pull my knit cap a little farther down over my ears. I can hear the train coming before I see it, clanking and thundering toward the station from the next suburb along the line. The commuters don't look up from their phones, but they begin to saunter automatically toward the place where they know the doors will pause and creak open in a moment. When the train slows and stops, I do my best to follow the commuters' smooth slide into the cars, but I'm awkward with my bags. I'm an obvious Metra newbie, taking up an entire middle seat, taking long sweeping looks around—too interested in this mundane activity to be a regular.

Around me, people stride down the aisles without smiling or meeting anyone's eyes. The train jerks to a start, and I watch a smart-looking young couple next to me take turns silently cleaning cat hair off each other's business suit with a lint brush, while at the other end of the train a middle-aged man with a beard, a flannel scarf, a messenger cap, and spectacles sits facing, but somehow never actually *looking* at, me. I find it jarring, this practiced, purposeful level of detachment. I put my own earbuds in and look out the window as the train rumbles and clangs along the tracks and the Chicago suburbs begin to bleed into one another, morphing slowly into city.

When was the last time I rode this train? Ten years ago?

Fifteen? I lean my head back against the familiar vinyl of the seat, and the metal floor rattles under my feet, and time fades away. I can remember being on this train at age fifteen, headed down to the city with a motley crew of spiritually devout friends to attend the Acquire the Fire conference—an event organized by an extreme youth ministry called Teen Mania and put on every year in cities across the United States. Was that the year I wore a chain of tiny gold safety pins and called it a necklace? I can't remember. What I *can* remember is the musty vinyl smell of this train. The thin veil of cologne and anticipation clinging to the air. The excitement rising in my chest.

Back then Acquire the Fire seemed like a microcosm of my own adolescent Christian faith. Or maybe it was the other way around—my life with God was a smaller, thinner version of that conference's electric worship songs, long desperate prayers, and earnest vows that culminated in teary-eyed huddles in front of the stage. I went every year. Every year I seemed to need it again— that shot of Light straight to the vein. It was how I inoculated myself against the things that I was working so hard to avoid: the desire for popularity, the pressure of peers, and, most of all, the predatory nature of my own worldly desires battling within me, trying to rip me away from Jesus.

As the train hurtled toward the city that long-ago fall night, smelling of sweat and Red Bull and Dream perfume by Gap, my chest tightened with expectancy. By the time we walked into the convention center, it was about to burst clean open. A worship team made up of attractive, guitar-strumming, angel-voiced Teen Mania interns sang power ballads of love to Jesus, and the room filled with smoke and light, the bass thumping, the whole group of us lit up by roving spotlights.

We were fourteen, fifteen, sixteen, wearing Abercrombie and American Eagle, toted in by youth pastors from the suburbs to this tent revival meeting for the new millennium. Those were the days when I could *feel God,* when he seemed as near as my own breath, the culmination of all my carefully crafted romantic notions—Jesus as Prince Charming, white-horse-grinning, rescuing his girl. And there wasn't a cynical or ironic bone in my body when I raised my hands in that crowd of evangelical teenagers, sang loud, called down heaven, asked God to *just be here now.* There wasn't a single open lighter in the place. Just us, swaying with our arms raised—glowing like ten thousand flames.

At the end of the worship set, the lights faded in, and our hearts were primed for the message. When the magnetic director of Teen Mania, Ron Luce, walked onto the stage, we applauded wildly. I can still remember that night's message in startling detail. I can remember the way that Ron Luce's voice filled the auditorium with challenge and authority as the sharp lines of his Texas-tanned profile filled the dual screens flanking the stage.

His message that night was really just a question: *How do you know that God is real?* He left the words hanging in the air, floating unanswered toward the ceiling beams, and then he sauntered down the steps and toward the audience. One by one he handed his microphone to the kids in the rows of folding chairs on the floor level. *Really. I'm asking. How do you know?*

Teens raised their hands, gingerly at first, then more vigorously. Ron handed the microphone to a tall, brown-haired boy, who took it and said, *Because the Bible says so?*

Okay, Ron Luce said. *But how do you know the Bible is true?* On the giant screens above, I could see the boy inhale while Ron Luce smiled strangely, as if he were waiting for a punch line that we didn't know was coming.

The boy stumbled over Sunday-school apologetics, hemmed and hawed toward an answer. *Well, the Holy Spirit . . . uh, he told people what to . . . how to write—* But Ron cut him off and took back the microphone to hand it to someone else. One by one he asked the kids the same question—*How do you know God is real?*—and one by one he poked holes in their half-baked arguments. He had an answer for everything they gave him, the master devil's advocate, and I was thankful to be way up high, out of reach of Ron and his microphone.

How do you know God is real? Ron Luce asked one final time, striding back toward the stage. We didn't know. We had proved that we didn't know. So Ron Luce told us.

Because you've FELT him, he said in a wild whisper. He walked from one side of the stage to the other, picking up momentum. *Listen,* he told us, and we listened with all of our hearts. *People can come up with an answer to every logical argument you can give them. But they can't argue with your EXPERIENCE.*

We waited with bated breath as Ron Luce explained that *this* was the answer that nonbelievers were really looking for. That every antagonistic comment would grow dim in the light of our ignited hearts, bright for Jesus, charged constantly by his presence. *This* is what would spark the spiritual "revival" that we were taught to crave in our high schools, our towns, our world. When Ron Luce left the stage and the worship band came back up in a cloud of artificial smoke, I stood with the rest of the auditorium, raising my arms, begging for God's presence.

So much of what I would come to understand about God and faith was being fashioned in the space of that weekend conference. *Better is one day in your court than a thousand elsewhere!* We sang it over and over again, an unending strung-out chorus, and I believed it, learned that when God was near, it smelled like artificial fog and sweat, like passion and urgency and falling in love. We fell to our knees, pushed down by the power of our emotions, asking God to come, to draw us, to pour out his presence, to *be here, be here, BE HERE.*

Later that night, as the train shot back toward the suburbs, I sat alone. The sound of my friends talking and laughing muted around me as I pressed my head against the window and looked out at the darkness. The thick glass felt cool on my face, still flushed with emotion—love and worship and passion, all of it coloring me crimson in the cool night air. I sat there and sang a worship chorus quietly, almost under my breath, the words fogging up the window. *You're all I want; you're all I've ever needed . . . help me know you are here.*

It was a song from the conference, one that we'd sung that night. It was a call for God's presence to crash in like a wave of light and illuminate the moment—and I felt desperate all over again. We were going home, going back to *real life*, and I felt my own awkward fifteen-year-old loneliness and the nameless ache of being young and unsure creeping in all over again. I needed to *feel*, in that moment, that God was still real. I sang the words over and over again, hoping that he might appear in the repetition, that the light of his love would come down into this train car and surround me like a spotlight.

I don't remember now if it did or it didn't. Perhaps that's beside the point.

The train lurches into the station, and I'm jolted into the present by the abrupt plunge into the dark underground of the Metra station and then by the howl of the brakes as the train comes to a stop. I shake myself out of the memory, but the tenor of it hangs with me as I shuffle toward the escalators in the damp underbelly of Union Station. It's Valentine's Day, I remember suddenly, when I see the vendors at the station selling roses and chocolates alongside the usual coffee and doughnuts and bagels. I take out my phone to text Andrew and see that he has already sent me one: HAPPY VALENTINE'S DAY! I LOVE YOU.

People around me are all on their harried way to somewhere else, heels and boots clicking sharply on concrete, staring past one another at the rest of the day. I lean against the side of the escalator so that they can climb past me while I type, I LOVE YOU, TOO. LOOK UNDER THE BED. THERE'S A PRESENT FOR YOU.

A beat . . . then the ellipsis that shows he's writing. YOU'RE THE BEST! I smile a little to myself, proud that I'd remembered to buy him that strategy board game he wanted and hide it under the bed before I left.

Outside, in the shadow of the tall buildings, the wind is subdued, its power tempered by the steel and glass rising around me. The Chicago River courses sharp through the city under bridges and between brick and glass. I can see my reflection in the giant store windows—tall gray boots, leggings, sweater dress, long puffy winter coat, knit cap. My hastily curled hair hangs long down my back; the duffel bag is looped across my body. I bear little resemblance to that fifteen-year-old girl who came down here again and again to *Acquire the Fire*. As if *fire* were something that could be collected, hoarded, held in your cupped hands.

To get to Alissa's apartment in Wrigleyville, I have to take the Red Line "L" train, which smells faintly of urine. I grip the metal pole, watching the commuters—another still life of anonymity as they sway automatically with the jerky movements of the train without ever looking up from their phones. The whole thing makes me feel lonely. It's not like I'm hoping for some stranger to strike up a conversation. But I still feel an eerily familiar kind of loneliness—the fragile vulnerability of finding oneself invisible among a crush of people.

You are here, the Nameless Something reminds me with its Cheshire Cat grin. *You have been here before.*

I shake off the feeling and look at my phone to see if Andrew has texted anything else, but he hasn't. I think about who else I could call at nine forty-five on a Friday morning but decide against it and turn off the phone. I don't really want to talk to anyone anyway. I just want to feel a little less alone, a little less out of my element, as I rock and sway with the jerking train as it winds through the buildings of Chicago. I trace our route on the map at the top of the car, mostly because it gives me something to do with my eyes. Chicago to Clark/Division to North/Clybourn to Fullerton. People get on and off, and a disembodied voice above reminds passengers to collect their belongings and watch their step. I smile and think of Alissa, who has left her wallet on the "L" train twice this month—and her mittens once.

Fullerton to Belmont. Belmont to Addison, where I push my way out the doors and move with the mob of strangers down the metal stairs into Wrigleyville. The baseball field looms on my right with its high stadium walls and classic red marquee: HOME OF THE CHICAGO CUBS. It's surrounded on all sides by souvenir shops and outdoor bars. In the spring and summer, the whole street buzzes with beer and brouhaha and *baseball!!* But today everything feels closed down and abandoned, made smaller somehow by the gaping winter emptiness.

Several streets past the stadium, I recognize Alissa's building by the familiar metal watering can that sits in the corner of her small balcony. I buzz in, and when I get to her third-floor apartment, the door is flung wide open, and she's bright-eyed and smiling under her fringe of brown bangs.

"Friend!"

"Hi." I sigh, dropping my bags on the landing and hugging her around the neck.

In the apartment behind her, the thin winter sun slants through the window and onto the exposed brick of her living-room wall. I squeeze her tighter and blink back the tears that spring to my eyes unbidden. There's something about it—the oldest, best kind of friend opening the door wide at the end of all that anonymity, all that Valentine's Day loneliness, all those lonely trains—past and present—crisscrossing suburbs and city, noisy and silent all at once.

I get drunk on Valentine's Day night in the accidental, too-busy-talking-to-notice-how-much-I've-had, drawn-out kind of way.

During the first glass of wine, Alissa and I talk fast. We're rushing through the last several months, tripping over the daily news of life. Her grad school. My kids. Talk of marriage leads to talk of sex, which transitions into lament about weight gain, followed by praise of food, then favorite recipes and food blogs.

I wander around the tiny apartment to look at the new additions since I was last here five months ago, right after her wedding. On this wall a framed photo of the whole bridal party in front of a Chicago city bus. On floating shelves in the bathroom, a display of city shots that she and her husband, Don, had taken one day on a date.

A black-and-white photo of the Metra catches my eye and reminds me of my train ride into the city this morning, with its poignant and haunting memory. "Did you ever come to an Acquire the Fire with me and my youth group? I can't remember," I ask, walking out of the bathroom and back into the kitchen.

"Random," she says, refilling her wineglass and sitting back down on the kitchen stool. "No. I was spared that particular kind of crazy. What made you think of that?"

"I don't know. Nothing. I was thinking about it this morning on the train."

She takes a sip and waits for me to go on, but I don't really know what it is I'm trying to say. It's not like I want to go back to those days. My evangelical girlhood, though I've left it behind, seems to be the stubborn and recurring theme of my life—not to mention in any writing I try to do. I have somehow become the reluctant owner of a *blog,* where I dink around with the old phrases—*On fire for God. Jesus Freak. Getting into the Word*—and try to find a way out from under them. I've been doing the work of prying up the old rotted-out boards upon which my faith was built; I've been trying to rebuild it on something a little more solid.

But the truth is, I can't seem to shoot the gap between what I thought faith was supposed to be like—look like, *feel like*—and what it actually is.

"I don't know," I say finally, sighing. I empty my wineglass. "It just used to be so easy to *feel God*." I roll my eyes as I say this, because I know it sounds clichéd. It's one of those lacquered Christian phrases that we stopped using a long time ago, right around the time we started saying *shit* and *damn*. But still, the thought of *feeling God* pulls at some tender place in my heart like a small, sharp fishhook catching, and I have to blink away unexpected tears and turn to refill my glass.

"God," she says wistfully. "I haven't *felt it* in a long time."

"Yeah." I think about the dark Minnesota mornings, the slab-heavy Bible. About feeling so full of emptiness as I press my back against the hard-backed kitchen chair, waiting. Then I take a long drink of wine. "Me neither."

During the second glass of wine, talk of feeling God gives way to talk about the trip I'm on with Dane and Liam—which leads us into nostalgic rambling about the Memphis road trip we took that Labor Day weekend all those years ago with Kim.

"Seven years? Could it have been *seven years*?" she asks.

I tally the dates on my fingers. "Six and a half."

"Six and a half," she repeats, shaking her head.

"I know."

"So the question is, will you be taking your boys on a detour to the *fabulous* Metropolis, Illinois?"

"Ha!" I say, sipping my red wine. "Um, no. I still can't believe we drove *two hours* out of our way to see the Official Home of Superman."

"How did we even find out about it?" Alissa wonders idly.

"I have no idea. I feel like it was something Kim knew about."

I think back to that tiny town in the cornfields with its fifteen-foot bronze statue of Superman in the middle of the square. Kim, Alissa, and I had stood there, thin and fragile and twenty-four years old, at the base of his legs, wearing overpriced Superman

T-shirts that we bought from the Super Museum at the end of our five-dollar tour. We'd asked a stranger to take our picture as we leaned together, posed and smiling.

Am I inventing meaning that never existed when I think that we were drawn there somehow? That we were all, in some way, needing to be saved? We were all fleeing our own burning wreckage that August—me, the ashen fallout of the Thing with the Coffee-Shop Guy, Alissa the sharp intersection of her own bad breakup and her parents' impending divorce, and Kim the numbing pain of a long-distance relationship with no end in sight.

"Do you remember how *sad* we all were that trip?" I ask. "I don't think I even realized it at the time, how much we were all just *falling apart*."

"I remember," she says softly.

I recall the way we confessed our secrets to each other. We purged our darkness, and then we passed Triscuits loaded with spray cheese and gas-station fountain Diet Coke back and forth like *Body of Christ broken for you, Blood of Christ shed for you*—a cobbled-together road-trip Communion, the only way we could take it. I recall standing in the shadow of that gigantic Metropolis Superman, posing for a photo, mocking the garish kitsch of it all, while simultaneously craving the romantic notion of being lifted out of our wreckage by a cape-wearing superhero and flown far, far away.

"I keep remembering that trip," I tell her, reaching for the bottle of wine to top off both of our glasses. "Honestly? I think it's part of the reason I'm doing this."

"This trip with the kids?"

"Yeah. I mean, I know it won't be the same. Obviously. But maybe it will be . . . something."

"I know what you mean," she says softly. "I think of that trip all the time, too."

I take a long drink of wine and exhale. "I thought I was done falling apart."

"I know," she says. She doesn't ask me to explain, and I don't know whether I could if she did. I just know that these last several months have made me brittle and afraid in ways that are so uncomfortable in their familiarity.

"Anyway," I say, "to the road!" I raise my half-empty (again) wineglass.

"And spray cheese!" she adds.

"And to Kim!"

"To Kim." For a moment there's only the sound of the clinking glasses, the passing city traffic below, the wind crying softly against the window.

We're well into that third glass of wine when we leave a slurry, indecipherable voice-mail message on Kim's cell phone. Sometime after that I go giggling into the bathroom to take a topless Valentine's photo for Andrew with my phone.

Alissa's husband, Don, comes home sometime between the end of that third glass and the beginning of the fourth. He has a bag of groceries from the Jewel down the road and plans to make homemade pizza for dinner.

"For my Valentines," he says, and he tosses a bag of Cheetos to the black faux-leather couch, where we're sprawled now.

"Babe," Alissa says gently, looking at the bag of Cheetos. "This is so nice, but just to let you know . . . these are not technically *cheese poofs.*"

He looks at us blankly. "They're Cheetos, right? I know they're off-brand, but a Cheeto is a Cheeto."

"Yes, but they're not the poofy ones."

"The poofy ones," he repeats, still not understanding.

She sighs. "There are two kinds of Cheetos. Crunchy"—she holds up the crinkly bag—"and . . . poofy."

"The poofy ones are pretty much all air and cheese dust," I interject.

"Yes," she says.

"You don't even have to *chew* them," I add. "They just sort of dissolve in your mouth."

"Those sound disgusting," Don says, taking out a pizza pan and setting it on the kitchen island.

"Disgustingly *amazing*," I say.

Don shakes his head. "You two will die at age forty-five, I hope you know that." I shrug, and Alissa unceremoniously rips open the crunchy Cheetos, which we pull out by the orange, dusty handful.

Don works on the pizza as we distractedly watch a DVR'd episode of *The Bachelor*. It's the Juan Pablo season, and I haven't been following the show at home because the crooning, Spanish single-dad/playboy annoys the hell out of me. But Alissa's been watching, and I'm always down for bad reality TV.

"There's eight beautiful women. Ay, ay, ay," Juan Pablo says as his helicopter flies over a panorama of New Zealand. "It's time to take things to the next level."

In my hazy state, I'm finding it hard to differentiate between the bawling, buxom blondes. "I don't know any of these girls. Who do we like?"

"That's Andi," Alissa says of the stunning brown-haired woman who has just scored the first date with Juan Pablo. They're on a speedboat, hurtling through some exotic New Zealand gorge, she flawless in a low-backed one-piece, he shirtless and grinning into the wind. "She's an attorney or something. I think. Anyway, I kind of like her." Andi follows Juan Pablo through a tight water passage toward what will turn out to be a hot spring and waxes poetic about learning to trust a man.

"I hate it how they make everything a metaphor for 'learning to be in love,'" I slur. "Or do I love it? I can't tell."

"Love is like a secret hot spring," Alissa croons. The camera zooms in on Andi, who wonders if what she's feeling is *real*—if this man could actually be her *husband*—and Alissa says, "Gag me."

"Tell me about it," I say, but I'm noticing the calculated beauty and romance of the date that has been arranged for them. The perfection of the whole thing is so complete that it rings false, but it's a foolproof backdrop for heightened emotions—for the pink-tinged feeling of *love*. It's possible that the girl named Andi knows this. If she *is* an attorney, it's likely that she understands the filtered fiction of all this—the carefully planned dates, the exotic location, the boy himself, with his defined pectorals and thick Spanish accent and suave television persona. It's a careful manipulation, and I'd be willing to bet that she *knows this.* But she gives herself over to it anyway. Andi takes Juan Pablo's hand and allows him to lead her into the secret hot spring—so desperate, I think, to *feel something* that she doesn't much care anymore if it's contrived or not.

"Don't do it, Andi!" I slur at the television, knowing in my heart that I probably would've followed him, too, just for that sudden powerful fluttering of winged feelings—real or not.

Don comes over with our pizza then, a plate balanced on each hand. "Valentine Number One," he says, handing me my plate. "And Valentine Number Two," he says, giving Alissa hers.

"Hey," she says. "I'm your wife. How am I Valentine Number Two?"

"I'm Valentine Number One, I'm Valentine Number One," I say in a singsongy voice.

Don slides down and puts his arm around his wife, and I miss Andrew.

"Is that a hobbit house?" Don asks, looking at the TV. We've transitioned into Juan Pablo's "group date," where a gaggle of highly touched-up women is wandering bewildered into the *Lord of the Rings* movie set.

"I think so," Alissa says.

"I feel like this is a weird group to bring to Hobbiton," I add as the runway-model-size women duck, one by one, into the tiny round house.

"This is *awww-some*!" one of the girls croons.

Alissa points drunkenly at the TV. "That's Chelsie? I think? Wait, no. Maybe Christy?"

"Mmm," I say, finishing the last of my pizza and putting the plate on the table. The room is feeling spinny and star-spangled from the wine, and I rest my head on the decorative pillow on the couch.

"It's time to take things to the next level," Juan Pablo says, one more time in earnest, broken English.

"I'll bet it is," Don says dryly.

I close my eyes for just a moment, and then I'm asleep on the couch and dreaming about roses and hot springs, about Ron Luce bursting into a flaming, giant statue of Superman. Dreaming about the road, stretching endless and empty—always ahead of me, always turning just out of sight.

Chicago, Illinois, to Indianapolis, Indiana

Sunday, February 16, 2014

In the fifth row from the front at the far left side of Deerbrook Evangelical Free Church on Sunday morning, everything looks pretty much the same as it has for the last fifteen years.

This is the church where my parents met, where I was born into the waiting arms of the Young Marrieds class, into Awana programs and Sunday school and Bible "Sword Drills" and love. The metal pipes of some long-gone organ still slant elegantly down the stone wall at the front of the church, although they're mostly hidden now by two giant projector screens.

The whiplash of it is jarring. Last night, at that funky Lincoln

Park bookshop, I was reading to a small audience about the faith of my youth. I stood before a giant magazine display, directly in front of a magazine called *Bitch*. (Before the reading, Alissa had casually hidden that magazine's cover. "You didn't need *that* headline right above your head while you read," she'd whispered.) I'd been holding a glass of wine in one hand and my book in the other and grinning nervously across the trendy, book-filled shop. Just last night, I'd been reading about this church, this life, my memories from when this was home. Now I'm sitting here in gray skinny jeans and a white sweater, feeling fifteen years old and thirty all at once.

The projector screens at the front of the sanctuary show the words of worship songs I don't know anymore. I don't know the people on the stage leading the songs either. Gone is the tall, stocky worship pastor with the hooked nose. Gone are the Swedish piano player and the church choir and the young drummer—the one I used to lecture about his swearing.

The pastor gets up to give the sermon, and it's not, to my surprise, the new head pastor—a former New York football coach with a gruff Mafia-esque voice. Instead it's a balding, dynamic black pastor with a broad smile and a suit.

"Who's he?" I whisper to my dad.

"Teaching pastor. Charles Johnson. Working on his Ph.D. over at Trinity." Dad's lips barely move when he tells me this in my ear. "He, Lou, and Tim trade off giving the sermons." His gray beard prickles my cheek as he explains. I can smell his Old Spice cologne and feel the crispness of his white button-down shirt, and I feel like looping my arm through his and falling asleep on his shoulder instead of paying attention. There's a fifty-fifty chance he would let me.

"I see," I say instead. I look down at my church bulletin, where I learn that the sermon series is Valentine's Day–weekend-appropriate. *Our Love Relationships,* it's called, and today's sermon is "What She *Really* Wants: Into Me See." The

Into Me See, Pastor Charles explains, is a slowed-down version of the word *Intimacy.* I try to listen, but I'm bothered by the weird grammar/pun in the title and oddly homesick for the short, balding pastor who'd led the church for as long as I could remember. Whose stories and anecdotes had become, over the course of hundreds of sermons, as familiar to me as my own.

The memory of Pastor Wally sends me backward-plunging into the Deerbrook of my youth until I find myself drowning in it. I can feel it like water around me—the first thrilling waves of spiritual fervor, the bright pure blue of first love, the weedy underworld of church politics and manipulation and fear not yet brushing the bottoms of my feet.

I sat with my friends in the front row back then, when the sanctuary was full of pews instead of chairs. We sat there because our youth pastor had told us we should. *Imagine if the youth of this church were so* on fire for God *that they sat in the* front row? *If they actually* led *the church in worship instead of slinking out the back?* We'd taken it as a challenge—a few of us, at least—and I'd spent four years of Sundays right in front of the carpeted steps of the stage, the boy I thought I loved on one side; my youth-group friends, clothed in American Eagle T-shirts and flared, stone-washed jeans and choker necklaces, on the other. I was convinced we were leading some sort of movement, so I took notes in my church bulletins and then stuffed them into the pocket of my black, Jesus Freak Bible cover, where they cataloged the growth of my spirituality week by week.

"The teacher in Proverbs says it like this," Pastor Charles exclaims suddenly from the pulpit. "Let her breasts fill you at all times with delight!" His awkward breast reference punches through the underwater quiet of memory and slams me back down in the fifth row from the front of present-day Deerbrook—far left side. "Be intoxicated with her. Be out of your mind. Be high with her love. *Can I get an amen?*"

The Deerbrook folks laugh gently. They are not raucous

amen-ers, but they are not too uptight for a polite, collective chuckle. I shift on the upholstered wooden church chair and look around at them. The people I used to know have almost entirely disappeared, replaced by mostly unfamiliar faces. The kids I used to babysit for have all gone off to college, and their parents have found other church homes. I don't know where the parents of my youth-group friends have gone, but it's not here in this winter-bright sanctuary. I recognize only two people: Linda, the willowy, gray-haired former Barbizon model, still wearing stilettos at eighty-something, and her husband, who seems to have lost a good amount of his hearing.

It's a strange thing—to find oneself a stranger in such a familiar place. Dad passes me the roll of wintergreen Certs that he always keeps in his pocket on Sunday mornings, and I unwrap it enough to pull one out and pop it into my mouth, where it tastes sharp and familiar and cool against my tongue.

"Somewhere along the line, somehow, we've allowed the fire to just kind of dim down," Pastor Charles says now, and he's talking about marriage, but his reference to fire dimming down makes me feel simultaneously guilty and defensive about things that have little to do with my marriage and everything to do with my formerly fiery faith itself. When he begins the numbered-list portion of the sermon—"Six Possible Results of Passionless Relationships"—the word *passionless* glows on the screen like a blinking red arrow, pointing straight at me. I glare back at it for a while before turning away from the sermon and toward the tall, thin window in the brick wall.

Outside the window Lake Cook Road rushes east toward the lake, connecting the moderately wealthy Deerfield community to the glittering, stone-walled mansions of Waukegan and Glencoe and Lake Forest, to Lake Michigan itself, most of its lakeshore privately owned and docked in the summer with million-dollar sailboats. How odd and tinny it sounds, to talk about passion—or lack thereof—here, in the middle of a polite suburban church, in the middle of a strip mall, in the middle of the affluent Northwest Suburbs.

Even in my Jesus-freaky growing-up days, passion was something we went elsewhere to find. The youth-group calendar seemed to take into account an inevitable fading of faith in the midst of too many normal days, and so the years were punctuated by conferences and retreats and concerts—a dozen opportunities for your faith to be fanned back into flame.

In the fall, of course, we boarded that train bound for Acquire the Fire. In wintertime a giant, double-decker bus called the Lightrider picked us up in the sloping church parking lot and toted us down to Florida, where we played Ultimate Frisbee on the beach and prayed aloud together by the ocean. In the spring we took fifteen-passenger vans to off-season Christian camps for youth-group retreats, where we spent our days rock-climbing and zip-lining. The dark, star-studded nights we spent singing dulcet, echoing worship songs around the campfire while the fire lit the contours of one another's faces bright.

And in between all of it, there was a smattering of Christian rock concerts, where we crushed into the crowds, waving our arms, singing along at the top of our lungs, pushing to get closer to the stage, closer to the action. Closer to God.

I don't really know anything about this Pastor Charles person, and he seems nice. Truly nice. Even so, I narrow my eyes against him now, wary of anyone who tells me to "feel it more"—whatever "it" might be. Marriage. Faith. Pain. Happiness. I have known passion—that intense, driving feeling that ignites you on the inside, that makes you feel *so sure* about everything. Outside, the frozen-over February world is still and gray, and I don't feel God at all—not big and fiery, not small and steady, not anywhere. Not near to me at all. Silent as the snow-crushed world around me.

In the fifth row from the front, at the far left side of the Deerbrook sanctuary, I feel emptied out and numb and tired. After church we will get into the car and drive south—the next leg of the trip. I don't know what I'm looking for, but it's certainly not the fiery curls of passion. It's something more substantial, more filling than all that. A different kind of light from the kind that so easily burns out.

The church service ends with a happy-clappy worship song, and I gather my purse and my empty paper coffee cup and trail out of the sanctuary behind my dad. The repeating worship chorus follows us out and spills into the church foyer, where people are gathered already in little pods of small talk, blooming out toward the center until the whole place is a kind of garden of smiles and laughter.

"Addie! So great to meet you!" someone says, and I don't know who she is but try to conjure up the kind of smile that says I might. "Your mom talks about you all the time!"

"Good things, I hope?"

"Oh, don't be silly. *Great things.* And those *boys* of yours. Adorable! I know Grandma misses them lots." The woman is small and highly coiffed and dressed in what looks like something out of a J.Crew catalog.

"Thank you." I smile and then try to gently extract myself. I look for my dad, who might be capable of making an introduction, but he's disappeared in the crush of post-sermon fellowship. "I should probably go get them—"

"Your mom tells me you're going on a trip?" The woman is not picking up on my subtle conversation-ending cues, so I acquiesce.

"Yes," I say, with what I hope sounds like enthusiasm. "I'm taking the kids down to Florida for a few days."

"Well, that's *brave* of you, isn't it?"

"I don't know about that."

"Oh, trust me. You are one brave lady!"

I nod politely, but it feels disingenuous. I have few illusions about being *brave*. I know that I'm not the first mother to do something like this—to hit the road, alone with her kids—and I won't be the last.

I read once about the first woman to drive across the United States coast-to-coast without a man. She was a twenty-two-year-old housewife and mother from Hackensack, New Jersey. She left her kids, and she drove. Only 152 of the 3,600 miles she drove were paved. It took her fifty-nine days and eleven tire changes—which she performed herself. I don't know the first thing about changing a tire, but I have a AAA card and a cell phone. I have a cooler full of Diet Coke and juice boxes and a paved eternity and a McDonald's every five to seven miles from here to Florida.

I feel like saying this to the stranger in the hall, trying to tell me I'm brave. Trying to tell me that I'm something that I'm so clearly not. I am a coward, running away from a perfectly beautiful life. If perseverance is the work of staying in the difficult place where you find yourself, then I am a failure. I am opening automatic minivan doors with the buttons on my key fob and then shutting them tight against the familiar world. I am turning on one movie after another on the dual monitors of the cheap car-DVD player to lull my kids into a passive, zoned-out obedience.

This is a First World kind of adventure.

This is a First World kind of escape.

By the time I've collected my kids from their respective Sunday-school classes, woven through the minefield of strangers-who-know-us, and hugged my parents good-bye, I'm wrung out and exhausted.

I hastily make up sandwiches for Dane and Liam in the church parking lot, turn on a movie, and get gas at the Shell station next door, where the youth-group bad boys used to buy cigarettes. Then we begin the long arc around Chicago on 294, past the airport, pulled along by the aggressively fast traffic around us. "Chicago Lead Foot," people used to call it. When I moved to Minnesota, I couldn't believe how politely people drove, keeping a cordial distance, ambling along the highway, waving each other in when the lanes merged. Here, at my sensible eight miles an hour over the speed limit, I am ticking people off left and right. They're roaring up to our minivan, flicking their blinkers impatiently, zigzagging around us. As I putter alongside those giant, bullying SUVs, I am extra aware of my essential minivan-ness in a sea of fancy, powerful cars. I pick up the pace just a little bit.

The sky is the same color as the exhaust-stained snow on the side of the road, and every hundred feet or so there seems to be another billboard. They're so close together that I feel almost dizzied by the colors, the messages, the sheer volume. Handsome men model thick, expensive glasses for Pearle Vision. Hot-N-Ready pizza is only five dollars. That bank has free checking. That hospital is apparently your best shot if you find yourself battling cancer. And if all else fails, there are plenty of casinos and strip clubs with eternally young, pouty-lipped models, giving that come-hither look to those trapped in their cars below.

Nearby universities have a host of billboards featuring studious and attractive young students and inspirational quotes about education. A sleek lawyer with a terrible comb-over leers large from his poster, promising to help you if you find yourself at the wrong end of a liability suit. ABC is working overtime to make sure you catch their brand-new show *Resurrection*. They've got dozens of black billboards, each with the same scrawled red text that says DID I REALLY DIE?

High above me businesses elbow one another out of the way with their giant ads until I can't stand to look at them anymore. I look instead at the people in the cars next to me, feet filled with Chicago-made lead, staring straight ahead. They are lost in their own insular worlds, hidden behind their car windows, driving, driving, driving.

❖

When we cross into Indiana, the first thing I see is a giant billboard that says HELL IS REAL in bold block letters. On cue, Liam starts crying and doesn't stop for over an hour. It's throaty and guttural and angry, punctuated with screams. *"Hold you! Hold you!"* The passenger seat shakes as he kicks it, and his face is red and tear-streaked and snot-soaked and furious. The only thing that seems to calm him down is if I reach back and hold on to his foot, which I do for several miles—my body angled and stretched impossibly between the steering wheel and the two-year-old sitting behind the passenger seat.

The movie's not working. They want *snacks.* Dane dropped the small stone that he stole from the landscaping at Deerbrook today, and he wants it *now.* When I let go of Liam's bare foot to try to grab it, he emits a shrill scream of protest. *"Hold you! Hold you! Hold you!"*

"ALL RIGHT!" I holler over their voices, and then I rub at my temples with my free hand.

They don't quit. If anything, they only scream louder. I pull off the road briefly at an exit, put on my hazard lights, and fumble my way out of the car to turn on a new movie, grab Dane's rock off the floor, and distribute snacks. The whining continues as I pull back onto the highway—but at a softer volume and at more acceptable intervals. I crank up the music on my iPod, grip the steering wheel, and try to focus on the lyrics and melodies instead of on the boys.

The phone rings—Andrew.

"I'm turning around. I can't do it."

"Oh, no. Presh."

"The crying is breaking my brain. My car-organizational system has completely dissolved. Is it okay if I ditch the van in Indy and fly us all home?"

Andrew laughs, and it's thick and drowsy at the edges.

"You just woke up from a nap, didn't you?" I say dryly.

"No," he lies. "Well . . . maybe."

"For your information I slept in a *trundle bed* last night. *With Liam.* Where's *my* nap?" Ahead of me the road to Florida stretches long and flat, and frustration wells up in me like bile, and it occurs to me that this is why people keep saying I'm brave. By "brave" they actually mean "crazy."

"Maybe you'll get one at Luke and Sarah's?"

"Doubt it."

"It'll get better," he says.

"Maybe." Around me the road is filled with travelers, all of them going *somewhere.* Driving. The snowbirds with their tight white curls and small dogs pressed up against the windows. The family vacationers in newer and fancier minivans than mine, arcing toward various Disney World resorts. The wanderers and escapees. The semi drivers, with their loads of merchandise to be unloaded in the stockrooms of Walmarts and Targets and grocery stores across the countries. We have set our speedometers to cruise control, hands on the steering wheels but not so much *steering* as simply staying in the lines. Letting ourselves be pulled by the road itself.

"I wish you were here. Fly down to Florida and meet us."

"I definitely would . . . but I have that interview."

I sigh. Andrew's been trying for the last several weeks to find a way out of his current, soul-numbing job into a new one somewhere else—and finally, things are starting to look promising. "I know. It's fine. I'll be fine."

"I miss you," he says. "Marty misses you, too."

"Oh, Marty-dog. Give him a kiss for me."

"He took a pee on the bed yesterday."

"What? No he didn't."

"Yes he did. Just on *my* side. Where *I SLEEP.*"

I'm laughing now in spite of myself.

"Yeah. He looked sheepish when I got home from my parents' house, but I couldn't find anything. Until I went to go to bed. And there it was. Big splotch of urine."

"I'm dying," I say. "What did you do?"

"I couldn't deal with it. I went and slept in Liam's bed instead," he says, and I can picture it, him grabbing his pillow, glaring at the dog, and then marching to Liam's room to curl his muscular adult body under the basketball sheets of the twin mattress that's currently sitting frameless on the floor.

"He's being passive-aggressive because you're gone and you're his favorite."

"I am his favorite. It's true," I say. There's a screech in the back, and I look at the rearview mirror in time to see Dane arc his arm back and smack Liam across the head. *"HEY!"* Liam shrieks.

"Dane!" I whisper. "We do *not* hit."

"But he was bothering me!"

"I don't care. You don't hit."

"Sounds like it's a fun time in there," Andrew says.

"It's a hoot." For a few minutes, I air my niggling complaints while he listens. So much fighting. So many questions. And *sleep.* I'd trade my left eyebrow for a full night of sleep without a kid sprawled over my numbing arm.

"You can do it," he says gently. My "Okay" is dripping with sarcasm, but still, I feel a little better after I hang up the phone and drive, drive, drive.

When I get sleepy, I crack open a lukewarm Diet Coke and put in the first disc of *Loving Frank,* the book on CD that I borrowed from the library a few days ago. The *New York Times* bestseller is a fictionalized account of the mistress of Frank Lloyd Wright—a detail I'd missed when I reserved it. But by the third chapter, it's clear that Mamah's marriage in all its ordinary goodness is not enough for her, that the young architect working on her garage is about to become so much more, that she is dancing crazily at the brink of her life, about to go off the edge. The whole story line brings back memories of my own near-miss affair, and regret settles like a bad taste in my mouth.

I sigh and flip the button to switch over from Mamah and

Frank's impending affair to the radio, where I scan until I come to a station that's not fuzzy. A Top 40 station is all I can find, and "Say Something," that hit song by a band I don't know, is on again. I let it play as I approach Lafayette from the north.

Say something, I'm giving up on you, the voice on the radio sings. And I know it's not a song about God, but I find myself there anyway, at the silent center of my faith, listening for something. *Anything.*

The pastor's voice from this morning comes back to me, reverberating baritone in my ear as I drive. *Somewhere along the line, we've allowed the fire to just kind of dim down.*

Is that it? Did I *allow* this to happen? Did I miss some important turn on my faith journey? Am I lost in this endless snowscape because of something I did or didn't do?

I can't believe that this could possibly be it. I think back to that girl, journaling in Caribou Coffee all those years ago. No one wanted *God* more than she did—sitting there in the faux leather of that chair, waiting every morning for him to ignite some ordinary object like a burning bush. Waiting for him to say, *I'm here, I'm here, I'm here.*

I'm not that girl anymore, but sometimes it feels like I'm still sitting, waiting. Still trying to find the thread that will lead me back to a faith I can feel.

Say something, I'm giving up on you.

Around me hundreds of tall, stately windmills rise up from the white fields. They stand in perfect rows, like sentinels, watching silently as we pass. At the towering tops, three thin arms are stretched out into the cold, turning, spinning the icy wind somehow into warm, pulsing energy. I duck my head to peer at them from the bottom of the windshield until they disappear.

The windmills fade behind me, and Liam starts crying again. I feel neither strong nor weak, neither here nor there as I speed through the heart of Indiana farmland. Reaching back and grabbing his small foot, I'm rooted to both my child and the steering wheel. Split down the middle, holding both at once.

INDIANAPOLIS, INDIANA

Sunday, February 16, 2014

Indianapolis is called "The Crossroads of America" on account of the several major highways that merge and connect and crisscross at its humble heart. "Naptown," "Circle City," "Indy," "The Racing Capital of the World"—all I really know of this city are its monikers, and I learn little else as I approach from the north.

There's a billboard for a children's museum that we don't have time to go to but that looks like all kinds of fun: a giant fake dinosaur propped against the side of a huge building, peeking underneath the roof. There's also an impressive amount of Starbucks logos on the blue FOOD and LODGING signs that rise up from the snowy netherworld on the shoulder of I-65. But that's where my introduction to Indy begins and ends. I don't even get a glimpse of the skyline before I turn off the interstate and into the Indianapolis suburbs.

We have already driven more than ten hours south, and still there seems to be even more snow here than there is at home. On the way into the subdivision where Luke and Sarah live, I disbelieve the speed limit and smack into a giant speed bump, half hidden by smashed-down snow. The whole van heaves and bottoms out on the ice with a sickening crunch.

"Mom! What was that?" Dane asks.

"Indianapolis," I mumble.

We met Luke and Sarah Kelly a decade ago during that gap year between college graduation and real life, when Andrew and I taught English in a small town in the southern part of China. Another stupid decision that people called brave.

Luke arrived in the factory town of Pinghu just a few days after we did, a week before the other American teachers would come. For those first sweltering summer days, it was just the three of us in a whole unfamiliar new world. We wandered together along the streets of Pinghu, exploring, ducking into tiny restaurants, getting our bearings. When the days became too hot, we'd sit on the linoleum floor of the still-unfurnished flat that Andrew and I had been assigned and watch movies on our laptop while playing three-handed euchre. From the top of the unpainted drywall above us, the A/C cranked loudly, working to cool the hot sixth-floor apartment.

Luke was already engaged to Sarah then, but she was back home in Indy at pharmacy school. Late at night he called her long-distance, and they burned through phone cards one at a time. She came once to visit, and I felt an immediate connection to her midwestern kindness and her obvious cultural estrangement. She followed Luke along to all his favorite haunts and smiled easily, but I could tell that she felt much as I did: out of her element, out of place, lost in the flurry of language and tradition and ritual.

We never discussed it then, but there was a certain kindred spirit born out of our shared isolation. We were both in love with men who loved China, men who felt a certain amount of ease among her people and history. We, neither of us, felt that same thrumming romance pulsing in our veins. Instead we felt the sweat and the grime, tasted the difference in the Diet Coke that they sold out of tiny, hole-in-the-wall shops, got sick off the MSG lacing our noodles at the local restaurants.

When Sarah left to go back to America, I felt the lonely emptiness of that year cut into my abdomen, deeper and sharper than ever.

Now I hoist our Indy tote bag, along with a laundry basket filled with the miscellaneous, scattered Other Things we need, out of the van. Dane, Liam, and I troop up the snowy driveway and stand shivering on the porch of their snow-covered beige two-story.

It's Luke and Sarah's blond, three-year-old son, Oliver, who opens the door. He stands there on the other side of the screen, surveying us with his mother's big brown eyes for a good minute before Sarah finally comes up behind him and swings the door open to let us in.

"You made it!" she says.

"Barely," I groan. She hugs me, this friend I haven't seen in seven years. Her pregnant belly presses against my car-rumpled shirt, and I exhale with relief. *We made it.*

"So that 'Hell Is Real' billboard on the way into Indiana," I say to Sarah. We're in her kitchen now—me on the tall barstool at the island, her leaning against the counter, one hand on the orb of her belly. In the living room, the kids have overturned the entirety of Oliver's toy collection and are now busy with the stamps and the piles of scrap paper that Luke rescued from the recycling bin at his office. "That's intense."

"Oh, I know," she says, rolling her eyes. She doesn't seem to have aged much in the decade since I first met her in China. She has the smooth, porcelain face and full lips of a girl in a 1950s Coca-Cola ad—tall and thin, even with her baby bump, an all-American kind of beauty. "It actually says 'Jesus Is Real' on the back—but you'd never know coming into Indy from Chicago."

"Classy."

"Super classy."

"It smells really good in here," I tell her, taking a long breath of the kitchen air, which is warm and heavy and smells like vegetables and garlic and thyme and sautéed onions.

"Stew," she said. "Crock-Pot stew, so it's practically cheating. Will your kids eat this?"

I grimace. "I doubt it. My kids are the pickiest eaters on the planet."

"No problem. I have sandwich stuff."

"You're an angel."

"I'm a mom." Sarah shrugs. "Luke isn't eating with us. He's going to church small group tonight. But we're forgiving him because he promised to bring us fountain Diet Cokes from McDonald's on his way back."

"It makes me feel better about my choices to know that you're a pharmacist and you still drink Diet Coke while you're preggo. I tried to give it up during my pregnancies but never could manage it."

"The doc says I can have one a day." She shrugs. She's not the kind of mom who worries that aspartame will give her child a third arm. "And you know that my love for Diet Coke is undying. And that McDonald's Diet Coke is superior to all others."

"Of course," I agree. In the living room, it is eerily quiet, and I have a brief moment of concern that my children might be stamping the Kellys' living-room walls with permanent black ink. "I feel bad that you're missing your small group," I tell her. "Do you want to go with him? I don't mind watching the kids, and we can hang out when you get back."

"Nah," she says, looking at her hands. "I don't really mind missing it." She says it like a confession almost, like a divulged guilt—and I understand. I've felt the same complicated weight that is currently sitting on her shoulders. I find myself nodding and *mmm-hmm*-ing as she tells me about their *two* small groups—one from college, one from their current church. She doesn't feel connected to either one.

I nod again. *I get it.* There is a way you're supposed to do Christian faith as an adult in your thirties. It has a certain look to it, an outline, a template. It meets in sanctuaries and foyers on Sunday mornings and then, if you're really *serious,* in other couples' living rooms one evening a week for decaf coffee and dessert. Or, if you're hipper, Bible and beers. It's hands folded in your lap, reading a Scripture passage around in a circle, discussing the implications for your daily life. It's "sharing your struggles," and it's "doing life together," and "Into Me See"—except when it isn't.

I want to tell her that I *get it*—the terrible distance of those uncomfortably close living-room circles. The ones where you know you're supposed to fit—the ones where you feel like you're failing when you don't. Here is where the holy fire of your grown-up faith is supposed to be kindled, week after week, conversation after deep conversation, into something that you can *feel*. And I know what it feels like when it doesn't seem to work. Because that's mostly how it is for me.

I want to tell her that I understand. That we first became friends in China, mainly because we couldn't love what we were *supposed* to love. Couldn't fit where we were placed. And that there is a certain kindred feeling born of our isolation again, now, at her kitchen island in the sprawling suburbs of Indianapolis.

"Anyway," she says, taking the lid off the slow cooker to inspect the stew. "I think Luke should just stay home with us. After all, we have company. And it's so *gross* outside with all the snow."

"I know. I think I might have broken my van on that speed bump at the front of your neighborhood. I couldn't see it. *There's so much snow!*"

"Winter," she says, rolling her eyes.

"Winter," I repeat. And it's hard to know if we're talking about the weather now or about the grown-up Christian lives that feel so dead and cold around us. She says "winter" and I hear something about the landscape of faith that I find myself in. She says "winter" and what I hear is the deepest kind of question—the one that's been echoing in my heart for longer than I care to remember: *It's so cold. Do you feel it, too? Do you think we'll make it?*

I don't remember watching the opening ceremony of the Sochi Winter Olympics, though it must have been on in the days before I left for my trip, the fireworks and the flags heralding the start of the games on our flat-screen TV, the volume turned down so it wouldn't wake the kids.

Certainly the Olympics coverage has been playing in the background this whole time—in our own Minnesota living room, in various restaurants and bars, even in the McDonald's that we stopped at on the way down from Minnesota on Thursday night. Tonight I finally find myself sitting squarely before the Olympic games in the Kellys' minimally decorated living room, watching.

The Olympics are a kind of movement, an undertow, carrying the world through another winter that is dangerously cold, where there is no end in sight. And though I'm not a sports fan by any stretch of the imagination, I find myself zoned in to the coverage as I sit next to Sarah, eating birthday-cake-flavored Oreos and sipping from the large fountain Diet Coke that Luke did indeed bring us from McDonald's.

In the Middle East, the Syrian civil war is spilling into Lebanon, and tensions are high in Somalia and Ukraine. There are brush fires in Australia and landslides in Burundi and senseless acts of violence everywhere. There is so much that does not make sense, so many narratives that circle and spin and never seem to resolve—my own included. But in Sochi the big story is NBC's official Olympics newscaster, Bob Costas, who has benched himself from his anchor position because of a nasty case of pinkeye that's left him swollen and painful to look at behind a pair of horn-rimmed glasses. An uneasy Matt Lauer has taken his place as the emcee, the voice behind the action, the narrator of the scrubbed and polished backstories of each Olympic athlete.

Sarah and I are next to each other on the couch, Luke in the armchair, the kids upstairs finally asleep under the floral bedspread in the Kellys' guest room. It took three trips back up the stairs and one trip out to the car to get the iHome before they finally settled down. I can still hear the muffled strains of the Slugs & Bugs *Lullabies* album pumping out of that tiny speaker upstairs, but otherwise everything seems quiet.

The coverage, which has up until now been detailing the various failures of American snowboarder Lindsey Jacobellis, switches to ice dancing. There is a short piece on Meryl Davis and Charlie White's *Two-Decade Road to Sochi*, which features the pair skating together as children and being super cute in old interviews: "When I'm skating by myself, sometimes I get nervous," Meryl Davis says in the old footage. She must be seven or eight. "It's a lot easier to have a partner with you all the time."

Now they skate out onto the ice—her in a purple sparkly halter-dress number with bejeweled collar, him with a shaggy mop of curly blond hair and a sharp nose. The violin music soars through the arena as they execute their dance, their arms strong and expressive. Him carrying her. Her twisting around his body. Curve. Lift.

"Oh, my goodness me," the commentator says.

"Look at that little hop into the twizzles," the other croons.

"Doesn't get more perfect than that," her compatriot agrees. And, not surprisingly, the duo wins the gold.

"*Twizzles* is my new favorite word," I say, grabbing another Oreo from the package.

"Get back to the skiing," Luke says to NBC.

The rest of the world's foremost ice dancers work mutely across the television screen, while Luke, Sarah, and I talk jobs and kids. For a brief moment, Luke wonders aloud what it might be like to quit his job altogether and work full-time with refugees, and I wonder if he feels it, too—the dull dissatisfaction of grown-up faith. The question throbbing under your numbed, winter heart: *Is this what it's supposed to be like? Is this all there is?* The question hangs in the air for one long moment. Then the ice dancing ends and the coverage fades out to the mountain rising snowy and glorious in Sochi's Olympic Park.

For a while we are quiet, watching the way the men cut down the mountain so expertly, leaning into the curves, riding over the snow. Bode Miller begins his run—the American favorite with the titillating underdog story: *Thirty-six years old—the oldest one there—whose younger brother, Chelone, died just this year. Seizures. He should have been at this year's Olympics, too, but Bode's here alone.*

We watch as Bode speeds down the mountain, weaving in and out of blue lines. He catches the air for a brief moment, and I wonder what it's like—to be carried like that, to throw yourself down an icy winter mountain . . . and to defeat it.

At the bottom of the mountain, the reporters are waiting for him, invisible vultures—voices behind the screen. A woman says, "This is such an extraordinary accomplishment, at your age after a turbulent year . . . to get this medal today. Put it in perspective for us. How much does it mean to you?"

He answers, but not to her satisfaction, so she tries again. "Bode, for a guy who said medals don't really matter—they aren't the thing—you've amassed quite a collection."

"This is a little different, I think—um . . . you know, my brother passing away," he concedes. "I really wanted to come back here and uh . . . race the way he would."

He's weepy, and she pounces on the first stray tear. "Bode, you're showing so much emotion down here. What's going through your mind?" She has an answer that she wants him to give, but he doesn't know what it is.

"It's been a long struggle coming in here. And, uh . . . just a tough year. And, uh . . ."

"I know you wanted to be here with . . . with Chilly really experiencing these games. So how much does it mean to come up with a great performance for him—and was it for him?"

"Oh, come on," Luke says.

"She's terrible!" I say.

Sarah nods with the straw in her mouth.

"Um, I mean, I don't know if it's really for him, but . . ." Bode tries. "I wanted to come here and, uh . . . I don't know, I guess make myself proud, but . . ." He trails off. She tries another question, but he can't seem to answer. He's red-faced, he's bending down, pressing his head against the metal handrail, and she's not leaving him alone. The video camera stays trained on him as he musters himself up, gets up and walks away from her. At a spot near the fence several feet away, he crouches down like a wounded animal, hunted and hiding.

"Well, that was . . . pretty much the worst," Sarah says.

"Yup."

We watch a while longer before we all start to yawn and run out of things to say. Then we say good night and pad up the stairs, disappearing into our respective rooms.

Later, when looking through pictures of the Olympic Games, I'll see a photograph of Bode by that fence . . . and his wife next to him. In the photograph she is holding his face, her blue-polished fingers against his helmet, the fur-lined hood of her navy blue puffer coat obscuring her face.

He can see it, though. You can tell from the look in his red-rimmed eyes that he can see it. That he is safe, he is *found*. That her face is telling him something he needs to know.

In the Kellys' guest bedroom, the boys are sprawled across the double bed, breathing steadily in the glow of the hall light. Neither of them stirs as I change into my sweatpants in the dark room or as I gently shove Liam over to make a sliver of space at the far side of the mattress.

From underneath the bedspread, in my tiny wedge of space, I look around the shadowed decor of the bedroom: mostly familiar souvenirs and artifacts from that year in China—delicate paper fans, unfurled scrolls, lanterns brushed with Chinese characters whose meanings I don't know.

I think about the Olympics, about the pushy reporter—a network-appointed tour guide through the tragedy of somebody else. I think about that skier, crouched in a ball at the edge of the fence, weeping.

Of course they picked on him. Who doesn't love the story of a person who has been destroyed . . . and then rises up to overcome? His story fits the American archetype about overcoming obstacles where the ultimate goal is to *get through* the Very Bad Thing and arrive on the other side. It's about sailing, strong and courageous, down that mountain toward victory and glory and a bright, shiny medal. Even in the Christian world, this sort of perseverance is a dominating narrative, and redemption is about a crossing over, a victorious leap over the void.

But that's not how I've experienced it. I am no conquering victor, no persevering athlete. My life fell apart once, and yes—there was a stunning moment of *grace* to be had at the clay bottom of the mess I'd made. But then it was mostly just a slow reassembling. A piecemeal recovery. There was no fifteen-foot bronze superman, sweeping me off of the ledge of my own making. It was a series of very small salvations: Marriage counseling. Therapy. *A husband who stayed.* There was the new-to-us house in the suburbs with ducks that arced overhead every fall and spring. There was the new (sort of wrong-for-us) church where I learned to let go of expectations. And then, at last, the new (sort of right-for-us) church. Small. Messy. Imperfect. A cotton swab dabbing at years of scabbed-over wounds.

Most days it feels like I'm still dealing with the same old struggles. Some days I feel so frighteningly close to being that most desperate version of myself—drunk-driving toward something that feels like *love* . . . but, of course, isn't. Most days I feel like I might—if asked too many questions—find myself curled into the fetal position by some fence, sobbing over all my unhealed places. Like a Believer who is still not really sure what it means to believe.

I sigh and kiss the top of Liam's head. It smells like sweat and peanut butter.

When my sons were born—two years apart, almost exactly—they split me open—all that love and fear, hope and terror, tearing through the center of me, making me a new person. It was a baptism of pain and loss, of blood and water, and when I held each of them for the first time in the fluorescent delivery rooms of Mercy Hospital two years apart, I felt two frantic feelings tangling together, becoming inseparable, being branded onto the soft, still-healing flesh of my heart: *Hope. Fear.*

Now I reach across Liam's sleeping body and brush my hand over Dane's cheek. He rustles and turns toward the other wall. *"We're okay,"* I whisper to myself in the darkness. *"We're going to be okay."*

The boys' breathing is steady and slow, and it steadies *me* as I lie in a tangle of my own unresolved faith in this unfamiliar room, in this ice-cold city in Indiana.

For a moment I think about nothing except for their breath, my breath, except for *breathe, breathe, breathe.* And then I am asleep.

Part II

////////

You can get lost on your way home.

You can get lost looking for love.

You can get lost between jobs.

You can get lost looking for God.

—Barbara Brown Taylor,

An Altar in the World

Indianapolis, Indiana, to Bowling Green, Kentucky

Monday, February 17, 2014

We've been on the road for exactly ten minutes, and Dane and Liam are already fighting. This time it's about sippy cups. They both want the blue one.

"My cup!" Liam screams.

"No, Liam! The blue one's mine! Because you had it last time!"

"My cup!" Liam screams again louder, still only two and lacking the language to create his own logical reasoning the way his brother can. "My cup! My cup! My cup!"

Dane reaches over the space between the seats and swats Liam on the head, and Liam lets out a shattering scream that works itself to the back of my brain and lights my head on fire.

"We do not hit!" I holler from the front. "Watch the movie, you guys!"

They glare at each other for a minute but, blessedly, turn back toward their screens to watch *Finding Nemo*.

I sigh. This is not how I imagined this going. At all.

The trip I'd concocted in my head was, admittedly, a parenting fantasy that I'd cobbled from Pinterest tutorials and movies and pure denial. The road trip I'd imagined was spontaneous and whimsical and colorful. Though it's true that I'd routed the trip along highways, I'd somehow still envisioned back roads. I'd imagined the three of us lined up at the Formica counter of a small-town diner, drinking milk shakes while some matronly waitress grinned a gap-toothed smile and leaned heavily on the counter to tell me all the local gossip. I'd imagined detours to places like Fairmount, Indiana—the hometown of James Dean—and Peru, Indiana, with its Circus Hall of Fame. I'd pictured us standing in front of the World's Largest Peanut and eating peaches sold from fruit stands in Georgia, juice dripping down our chins.

In this road-trip fiction, I am patient and fun-loving, gently pointing out roadside attractions while looking sun-dappled and relaxed in my sunglasses and loose curls and T-shirt. And the kids are dazzled and dizzied, running happily around abandoned circus grounds and historic graveyards before settling into a diner booth to gratefully eat their Blue Plate Special of two chicken strips and hand-cut fries.

As it turns out, I'm at the helm of our gray minivan, surrounded by string-cheese wrappers and sippy cups, cutting down a nondescript stretch of I-65. Just a few minutes ago, I had to actually unbutton my jeans because they were pinching my belly fat. My T-shirt is rumpled and full of dried chocolate milk from when Liam spilled all over me this morning during our breakfast with blog readers at the 3 Sisters Café. This is no one's road-trip fantasy—least of all mine.

The Indianapolis skyline appears briefly to the left of us and then disappears just as quickly, overtaken by the expanse of dormant farmland and the steel-gray sky that is heavy with rain and about to burst open.

The kids refuse any fast food but McDonald's, and although I have downloaded the Roadside America app on my phone, all of the interesting stops seem too far off the highway to be worth trying to find. The nearby ones are closed for the season, and anyway, it doesn't really matter, because all I can think about is *getting to the next stop.*

A trip has "personality, temperament, individuality, uniqueness," John Steinbeck wrote in his memoir *Travels with Charley.* "Tour masters, schedules, reservations, brass-bound and inevitable, dash themselves to wreckage on the personality of the trip."

If this trip has a personality, it's not the whimsical fairy godmother that I'd hoped for. Instead it's a dour, single-minded nineteenth-century schoolmistress, demanding that I *get there* as soon as possible. This trip does not want to linger or explore or dawdle along back roads. It is losing steam to the unexpected reality of Kid Time—the long minutes and hours surrendered to emergency potty stops, to public-bathroom hand dryers and gas-station candy aisles and rest stops with small swaths of mottled grass around which my boys *must run.* It's the time that disappears when I pull over to change out DVDs or grab a toy off the minivan floor or refill water bottles or get more string cheese out of the cooler in the back. Kid Time is turning my quaint, fun road trip into a single-minded mission.

This is how it happens that we end up stopping on Monday afternoon not at some fantastically unique roadside stop but rather at yet another McDonald's—this one at the southernmost tip of Indiana. The billboards promised that this particular McDonald's had a giant tree-house play area—the biggest one for miles—and that's really all I needed to know.

It's well after lunchtime and nowhere near dinner when we pull into the lot and launch out of the minivan, but I figure we can get ice cream. Here at the edge of the South, the snow is thin and dirty, barely covering the rocks, and I could swear that it's starting to feel just the slightest bit warmer. Inside, the cashiers all seem to have box-dyed hair billowing underneath their McDonald's visors, and their skin has the pallid look of years of chain-smoking. It's impossible to tell whether the women are thirty or fifty, but they call me "honey" in kind, textured voices and ask if they can help carry our heaping tray to the play area.

Dane and Liam sip their milk shakes for a minute or two and then abandon them for the plastic McTreehouse, and I crumble into a booth in the corner. At the tables around us, parents sit in pods of two or three. Their babies sit in gray sticky-seat high chairs pulled up next to them, while the mothers speak quietly, a slight southern drawl in their voices.

At home my own mama friends are picking up their kids from preschool, talking to each other in the hallways, shaking snow-flakes off their puffer coats, talking about the weather. It's not that I want to be there, slipping through the icy parking lot toward school and small talk. Not exactly. It's just that I feel so disconnected here, in this moment, alone in a town whose name I don't know. My boots squeak on the tan-tiled floor, which is littered with wilted french fries and the sodden remains of half-eaten Chicken McNuggets. The whole place smells of damp shoes and chocolate milk, spilled twenty times a day, sopped up again and again with the same gray mop and industrial cleanser.

Around me the mothers' damp hair is pulled tight in claw clips, and they bend over their drinks and talk quietly—*why so quietly?*—and I imagined this all *differently.* Me—connected to my kids in some new and beautiful way, connected to the road beneath us, the country and world around us. God maybe. Myself at the very least.

From the primary-colored play structure, I hear my kids laughing, their hands and knees banging up against the plastic as they crawl through toward the yellow tunnel slide again. From the speakers above me, Contemporary Christian music plays a song I vaguely recognize but cannot name. I stopped listening to Christian radio long ago, but I can still recognize it almost instantly by the chords of the guitars, the earnestness of the singers, the pink-tinged mood of the whole thing.

I log in to Facebook and write, *"They're playing Christian contemporary radio at the roadside McDonald's. Does that mean we're officially in the South?"* Over the years I've gotten good at writing these kinds of statuses—short and snarky, guaranteed to pique the interest of my blog readers. Most of them, like me, are still trying to figure out what faith looks like outside the glistening soap bubble of "Christian culture." The likes and comments come rolling in, and I feel less and more lonely all at once.

I text my mama friend and tell her I wish she were here. I text Andrew to see how his day is going. I imagine his face inclined toward his computer in his basement home office—his eyes squinting at the screen under his glasses—and sigh. I call the friend we're supposed to stay with tonight in Nashville and leave a message on her voice mail. "It's taking much longer than I thought," I say. From somewhere in the tree-house tubes, I hear Liam shouting, "Minja Turtle power!" over and over. "I'm not sure if we're going to make it to town, or if we're going to stop at a hotel somewhere. I'll keep you posted."

The rain starts in fussy little spits but soon works itself into a full-blown rainstorm. I stare at the big window next to me as the rivulets come down and wash into the patchy remains of snow. I lean my head against the vinyl back of the seat and watch the rain beat against the window, and it's probably going to be hell to drive in, but in this moment I don't care. I'm mesmerized by water on glass, by all that is being washed away.

It's the first rain I've seen in months. We are crossing over some invisible line between North and South here. We are getting closer to whatever it is that I'm driving toward.

I take surreptitious sips of Liam's milk shake, suck down the caramel-colored dregs of my Diet Coke, and holler to the kids that it's time to go. When they come tumbling down the tube slides, I touch the tops of their sweaty heads, tell Dane to use the family bathroom located in the play area, and then herd us all back to the car. I'm anxious to be back in the minivan, anxious to move on. The van has become my command center, my safe place, the center of my world on this trip. As long as I'm at the wheel, as long as my children are strapped into their seats, as long as we're *moving,* everything feels manageable.

But the rain comes fast and urgent, pouring gray sheets of water over the hood of the car as we drive, streaking down the windshield, making everything blurry. The windshield wipers are set to their fastest and most frantic, *swish-swish-swishing* at the water as I drive slowly with my lights on. I'm feeling for that place where the van's tires meet the asphalt, worrying constantly about losing my grip and hydroplaning. It's loud, the sound of rain on road, rain against the car and against the semis around us, spraying beneath their gigantic tires. "I can't hear the movie!" Dane whines, and I try to turn the volume up as loud as it goes without taking my eyes off the road. I can feel my shoulders seizing up with the stress of it all, my knuckles paling as they grip the steering wheel tight and the wipers *swish-swish* madly against the rain.

For one blessed moment, as we cross the big steel bridge over the Ohio River, the rain seems to let up. WELCOME TO KENTUCKY! a sign says. I try to take a picture through our rain-splattered windshield with my phone, but it comes out blurred and water-pocked.

Louisville rises small yet regal from just beyond the river—a crop of modest skyscrapers. Blue-glass windows and domed roofs and hotels—the whole thing refracted in the rainy turbulence of the river. I think about how all the skylines look both alike and different, and how if this were the trip that I wanted it to be, it would be sunny and I'd be wearing faded blue jeans and a flannel shirt. There would be jazz music in some park—a Louis Armstrong tribute band, maybe—and I'd buy the kids popcorn from a street vendor and take them on a riverboat ride, where we'd all turn a glowing shade of pink in a beam of unseasonably warm February sun. But as I drive over the bridge, the city disappears in a fresh dousing of rain, and so does the imagined detour.

We drive. The landscape changes next to us, a steep cliff of rock to the left of the car, green road signs and turnoffs at the right. Liam begins to scream, that heartbreaking refrain of *"Mama hold you!"* over and over until he wears himself out and falls asleep in midsentence, his head hanging like a broken limb. The rain starts, stops, starts, stops. Stops.

A green road sign on my right tells me that I'm coming up on Elizabethtown, and I almost drop my half-empty paper cup of Diet Coke. There is a quirky, independent movie of the same name that has been one of my favorites since I saw it in the theater with friends for the first time nearly a decade ago. It strangely never occurred to me that Elizabethtown might be an actual, real-life town, though now it seems obvious. Seeing it there, the sign for Elizabethtown suspended above the road like that, I feel it must be some kind of omen.

I call Andrew. "You'll never guess what town I'm passing."

"What town?"

"ELIZABETHTOWN!"

"No way. Is it Exit 60B?" he asks, citing the scene in the movie when Orlando Bloom playing Drew Baylor spends hours lost on the roads around Louisville looking for Exit 60B. He finally ends up parked next to a pasture in Missouri, sitting in his car, looking blankly out the window. *Did I miss 60B? Did I miss 60B? DID I MISS 60B?*

"Not 60B, believe it or not. Exit 61. Can you believe the movie lied to us?" I tell him. "Oh, I really want to stop."

"You should," he says. I nod as if he can see me, here in the Cheeto-dusted driver's seat of the minivan. I'm thinking about the movie now, the way a recently-fired-from-his-job and suicidal young man named Drew is forced to return to his hometown when his father unexpectedly dies. On the way he meets a quirky flight attendant named Claire who helps him through the inevitable emotional fallout of the next few days.

"I *should* stop. But it's raining. And Liam just stopped crying and fell asleep. I don't know if I can risk waking him up."

"You should stop anyway."

"It'll be nothing like the movie. It'll have really depressing things . . . like Burger Kings and Menards and Walmarts."

"Probably."

The ridges off the sides of the road are layered sandstone or siltstone, and the forested hills beyond them are rugged and woolly. I look at them, thinking about the final scenes of the movie. After the funeral plans finally culminate in a quirky and disastrous memorial service, Drew gets into his rental car for a spontaneous road trip home. Claire has made him a binder filled with maps and mix CDs and instructions. *Begin your journey and do not skip ahead,* Claire's voice-over says as he stares at the map, and so he sets out—the urn filled with his father's ashes buckled into the passenger seat next to him.

"This trip would be going much better if you'd created a road-trip binder for me like Claire made for Drew in the movie. *Where is my binder?*"

"I knew I forgot something."

"How am I supposed to know where to stop for the world's best bowl of chili? Or when to get out and dance with one arm raised above my head?"

"I guess you'll have to wing it."

"Yeah, yeah."

We talk a few more minutes, and then I hang up and drive past the exit for Elizabethtown with a mix of resolve and regret. I think about Drew, this fictional character who seems so real to me, driving through the varied topography of America. As he drives, he begins to release the ashes of his father, handful by handful. At tourist stops and historical landmarks. In the place where Martin Luther King Jr. was killed. At the base of the Survivor Tree in Oklahoma City. With one hand out the window, the ash slipping through his fingers and into the blue of field and asphalt and traffic. It makes me cry every single time—the beauty of that releasing.

But this is not a movie, and letting go is not a musical montage of charming moments. It's a much longer process, so much more dull and uneventful and *hard* than all of that. And if I stop in Elizabethtown, there's a chance Liam will wake up, start crying again, and never, ever stop, and I can't risk it.

I dig around the passenger seat for a few minutes, groping for my iPod so that I can at least turn on the *Elizabethtown* sound track. But my organizational system has totally collapsed, and although I spend at least five minutes digging beneath the spilling gifts and granola bars and empty pop cans and DVDs, the iPod is nowhere to be found.

I give up and turn on *Loving Frank* instead. The narrator, who's pictured on the back of the audiobook set, is a matronly looking woman named Joyce Bean. She picks up the reading where Mamah is boarding the Rocky Mountain Limited train with her children to visit her friend in Colorado. Not really visiting. *Fleeing*. She's just told her husband that she's in love with another man. With Frank. The scene of the confession replays in her head as the train carves its slow way west, and it makes me sad for this woman, this man—for all of us, our selfish hearts cutting one another in two as we run, run, run away.

❋

When I step out of the car at the Econo Lodge in Bowling
Green, Kentucky, the air is damp and heavy like a blanket strung
on a clothesline. But it's *warm*. A few last raindrops wring themselves from the sky as I pull the door open and let the kids out.

I'd hoped to make it all the way to Nashville tonight, but it's almost dinnertime, and I'm worn down like an old pencil. The kids
have gone from screaming with anger to screaming with silliness
so many times that my neck is stiff with the whiplash of it. The
rain hasn't helped, making otherwise perfect stops impossible.
Not fifteen miles ago, we passed a giant outdoor park called Dinosaur World that would have been ideal for a road break—both
"American quirky" and kid-friendly—except for the torrential
downpours around us. I didn't even bother pointing out the giant
plastic T. rex peering over the highway. I knew it would be futile.

So here we are in Bowling Green. I suspect that if I take this
exit in one direction or another, I'd probably find some charming little town of the type I've been hoping for. But I'm too tired
to even try. Instead I choose the first highway exit hotel I see—
the Econo Lodge. Across the street are a gas station and another
McDonald's, and the sign outside the big brown building prom-
ises a heated indoor pool. I figure it'll do.

I stand there in the empty parking lot of the Econo Lodge for
a long moment while the boys run circles across the broken asphalt, their shoes *slap-slap-slapping* against the ground. Before I
start unloading our totes and swimming stuff and toys, I pull off
my gray cardigan and look up at the great gray dome of the sky.
Somewhere behind it there is sun, and somehow that invisible sun
is warming the world around me. I stretch my arms wide and roll
my neck backward, and it feels like a kind of arrival. *South.*

Later I'll look at the weather app on my phone and see that it
was only actually fifty-eight degrees at that moment—not particularly warm, all things considered. But to my winterized nerve

endings, so used to the shattering cold of half a dozen degrees below freezing, it feels warm enough.

The lobby is empty when we walk in. "I need a room," I say to the young, smooth-haired girl at the counter. The boys bounce around the tables in the hotel's breakfast area as though it's a pinball machine. I add, unnecessarily, "One adult . . . two kids."

"One night?"

"Mmm-hmm." Liam whacks his head on the table he's been climbing under and lets out a wail. "Listen," I whisper conspiratorially. "Is there any chance you could give me some kind of free upgrade? Like . . . do you have any suites? With separate rooms?"

"Sorry, no," she drawls. "But I can give y'all a king-size bed with a little living-room area if you want."

A chair falls over with a terrible metal clank. "I'll take it," I say, handing her my credit card.

The Visa is one of those personalized ones, featuring a cherubic photo of the boys just after Liam was born. Dane is two, holding his baby brother for the first time, planting a gentle kiss on his infant nose. "Aww," the girl says, looking at it. "Cute."

I muster a small smile. Behind me Dane and Liam are kicking each other underneath a table. "Yeah . . ."

The laundry basket in my arms is loaded down: snacks, stuffed animals, blanket, laptop, toiletries, and the Nashville tote bag. A bottle of wine that I grabbed at the last minute from the bag of hostess gifts at the back of the van sits squarely on top. The giant blue IKEA bag filled with our swimming stuff is cutting into the crook of my arm where it is looped along with my purse. The bulky weight of all the stuff we need for just *one night* is staggering, and I set it down for a moment while the button-cute clerk drawls on about the weather and runs my credit card.

Near the counter there's a basket labeled with a sign instructing patrons to deposit any dirty rags and towels there. Later I'll learn that the basket is for the owners of the cars at the Corvette Museum across the street, where just the other day a sinkhole opened in the ground and swallowed up a million bucks' worth of cars. It will strike me as terribly poetic that I found myself stopped for the night at a place where the earth had worn so invisibly thin that suddenly it just gave out altogether. "All right, y'all," the girl says. "Here's your room key. Have a nice stay!"

In the elevator Dane and Liam jump up and down, laughing over their weight displacement while I juggle baskets and bags. "No, no, Liam," I keep saying, as his sticky little fingers gravitate toward the red alarm button. It seems to take an eternity for the door to open at the deserted second floor, but when it does, they go springing down the long hall in the late-afternoon sunlight that streams through the window at the end. "Come back!" I whisper-shout, but they keep going, too full of energy to stop, shaken cans of soda opened and running over.

In the hotel room that is decidedly *not* a suite of any kind, Dane and Liam jump up and down on the king-size bed, chanting, "Let's go swimming!" Over and over. The "living-room area" that the sunny clerk mentioned is a faded old pullout couch butted up against the nightstand, and the only "separate room" is the bathroom, where I try to barricade myself to change into my one-piece tangerine bathing suit. Dane and Liam fling themselves madly against the door. "Swimming! Swimming! Swimming! Swimming!"

"I'm coming!" I yell from the other side of the door, jamming myself into the spandex of the suit and pulling my hair on top of my head. What I really want to do is sit on the floor in total silence and cry for a while. But Liam is trying the doorknob now, letting out strangled, panicked sobs that he can't get it open. I splash a little cold water on my face, take a breath, and open the door.

"Who's ready to go swimming?"

It's a few hours later when Dane, Liam, and I find ourselves sharing an awkward, dripping elevator ride up to our room with the Little Caesars delivery kid. I'd called and ordered dinner from the echoing center of that dingy, dark pool room, the windows filmed over with residual winter grime. As I listened to the specials, I'd surveyed the imposing wheelchair lift and watched my kids kick across the pool, Puddle Jumper floaties looped around their arms and stomachs. When I'd ordered a pepperoni pizza and breadsticks, my voice had echoed in the empty cavernous room, and I could taste the chlorine seeping into the back of my throat.

The delivery kid is not more than eighteen or nineteen and is looking pointedly away from the drowned-rat-of-a-thirty-something mom in the tangerine bathing suit next to him. There weren't any towels in the pool room, so I don't even have the luxury of covering my thighs as the elevator creeps, shaking and lurching, toward the second floor.

I stare at the closed doors as Dane and Liam jump around us, sending excess water drops flying. *Come on,* I tell the doors. *Open.* When they finally do, I lead the pizza boy to our room door. I'm dripping and trying not to think about my undisguised ass wobbling as he follows behind us. When we get inside our room, I rummage through my purse for enough cash, which turns damp in my chlorine-creased hands by the time I hand it to him.

"Cold, cold, cold!" Dane is screaming inside the door, stripping out of his bathing suit, his bony white bottom exposed to the embarrassed delivery boy. Liam has crumpled into a heap on the floor, crying.

"Thanks," I say as I throw the money at the kid and shut the door in his face. I toss the pizza boxes on the laminate surface of the hotel table and hurry into the bathroom to run a bath. When they're both settled into the tub, I strip off my own suit, wrap myself haphazardly in a pilly white towel, and wander into the tiny entryway of our room outside the bathroom. I can see the boys through the crack in the open bathroom door, painting their faces with white hotel bubbles. I sink down onto the floor, knees pressed into my stomach, back pressed against the wall. It's as small as I can make myself without actually disappearing.

At the top of the laundry basket of stuff I hauled in from the van, the bottle of Green Fin Red Table Wine winks at me, and I grab it. Some hostess on our route will have to do without, but not me, not tonight, as SpongeBob SquarePants blares from the TV and the kids scream at each other in the bathroom—"Stop taking all the bubbles, Liam!"

All I have with me is the cheap waiter's corkscrew that I threw in my purse at the last minute. I don't really know how to use it— I'm used to the fancy bottle opener with the rising metal arms. I look at the curly metal tip and then jam it into the cork and pull. Nothing. I press my back against the wall, hold the bottle between my knees to try to get some traction, and yank some more at the stubborn corkscrew without success.

In the bathroom, water is sloshing liberally over the sides of the bathtub onto the tile floor.

"Don't splash the water, guys!" I grunt, still wrestling with the stubborn cork.

"Okay, Mom," Dane says. The water slaps against the tub, and I hear him say to his brother, "Look, Liam. This is how I swim *for real.*"

"Wow," Liam says, his voice filled with wonder. Then a crash of water against the tub, and he's screaming again. "No *SPLASH* me, Dane!"

I look at the wine bottle. My efforts have succeeded only in making the cork look ragged and broken and stuck. I knock the back of my head against the wall a few times in frustration and briefly consider whacking the bottle against the sink and breaking it open at the neck. *You are thirty years old. You have a master's degree, for crying out loud. You are smarter than a kitchen utensil.* I give the cork one more desperate tug, and it reluctantly budges— just a little. I take it as a sign.

I yank at it maniacally—*Come on, you sonuvabitch*—and then

it's out, leaving broken crumbles floating at the top of the marble-red wine.

The Econo Lodge only has flimsy Styrofoam cups, individually wrapped and sterile on the tray next to the ice bucket. I unwrap one and fill it to the top, skimming off the tiny cork remnants with my finger before taking my first drink.

There are people who could tell you whether this wine is good or bad—and why. There are people who can name hints of flavors and undertones and *notes* of wine, as if it is a song, a symphony, a hundred different instruments working together making something beautiful.

I am not one of those people. What I taste when I sip at the Styrofoam cup is not a kind of music welling up inside me but a medicinal kind of soothing—as if the wine is going straight to the frayed edges of my nerves and quieting them, deadening them, making the whole world a little fuzzier, a little quieter, a little easier to take in. I close my eyes. For a moment I can almost pretend I am at the bottom of the hotel pool and the world is soft and chemical-blue around me. I sit in the muffled silence, and for one blessed moment everything is quiet.

Inside the bathroom the water sloshes again, and I open my eyes. A small wave of bubbles breaks over the doorjamb between bathroom and hall and creeps toward me along the grain of the faux-wood flooring. I watch it and do nothing to stop its progress as it inches toward me.

Out the hotel window, the highway rolls by, and the glossy-postcard road trip I imagined we'd be having glides by with it. It's heading toward Florida without us. It's blowing a kiss out the back window and waving its silver-bangled wrist out the sunroof. It's a fictional, movie kind of road trip, an *Elizabethtown* montage of meaning and "World's Greatest Chili" and random dancing stops, and it isn't real. I know it isn't real. But still, I feel sad as I look out at the road, disappearing from sight.

My wine is not quite gone yet, but I fill the Styrofoam cup back to the top and then push myself up. I drop my damp towel and mop up the puddle of warm water on the floor with my foot, then put on some sweatpants. I take another long sip of wine, steeling myself for the next hour of dinner and bedtime in this small, unfamiliar room.

"Okay, guys. Time to get out of the tub," I call finally. "Pizza."

Nashville, Tennessee

Tuesday, February 18, 2014

Imagine that when you are twelve or thirteen or fourteen—at your most fragile and formative—you are taught to recognize "God's presence" by the fireworks you feel in your chest.

Imagine hearing, over and over, that faith is like a fairy tale, like a romance. *God is a relentless lover,* says your youth pastor and your Christian teen-romance novel and the May issue of *Brio* magazine and the inline devotionals of your Teen Life Application Bible. *Jesus is a Prince-in-Disguise who comes to the world to die, to rise again, to save you—his truest love.*

Of course, there are many ways to talk about faith, many

metaphors for God—but imagine that *this one,* this narrative, is the song that you hear on repeat for six, seven, eight years of your life. You are singing along with Jars of Clay in your car, "I want to fall in love with You!" and it's not a song about another person—it's a song about *God.* And, truth be told, you're already in love—head over heels, heart pumping with the sweetness of it, reading your Bible all afternoon in your twin bed while your peers are off exploring one another's bodies in theirs.

Try to imagine all this without the lens of cynicism, realism, or adulthood. Try to feel the bliss of it. *God loves you,* and *you love God,* and it's all-night worship concerts and genuine, crystal-line tears and long, cursive prayers that fill three dozen homemade journals. And *hope.* Try to imagine feeling a relentless, over-whelming sense of *hope.*

Then try to imagine it gone.

Imagine that magical, dewy first love evaporating, slowly at first, then all at once. Imagine that you're sitting in the gray cu-bicle of some IT company, feeling yourself fading into the walls, fading away from yourself and everyone you love.

Imagine desperately trying to rekindle whatever passion it was that you once felt for God. Imagine opening your Bible—which you'd once felt was a *love letter just for you*—and finding it to be a concrete slab in your lap. Imagine trying to talk to God, who you'd always felt was your true love, and finding your voice bouncing against the rafters in the coffee shop. No answer. No light. No fireworks. Imagine.

This is where I found myself the summer that I turned twenty-four.

Before there was that near miss of an affair with that graphic designer at the coffee shop, before the whole thing fell apart, there was just this: just this concrete quiet—just this gray heaviness.

And then, early that summer, I attended the annual Society for Technical Communication conference. It was a two-day ordeal held downtown at the Minneapolis Convention Center, complete with swag and sessions and schmoozing. I dragged myself from one boring panel to another with my notebook and pen, feeling scraped up and susceptible for no reason I could really name.

At one particularly boring session on single sourcing and localization—the room dark and packed full, the PowerPoint slides filled with information so dully incomprehensible that it made my brain hurt—a man sat down next to me. Out of the corner of my eye, I noticed him give an overt, undisguised double take, and if I'd been smarter or stronger or less banged up on the inside, I might have gotten up and found another spot right then. But I didn't.

How it was that we began scribbling notes on the bottom of my notebook, I don't remember. Perhaps he asked a question about the content? Or made a comment about the speaker's bad jokes? Whatever started it, the volley of handwritten snarkiness entertained me for a while until eventually the stranger paused . . . and scratched out an invitation at the very bottom of the lined notebook page. *"Have a drink with me after?"*

I'd paused. *"Married,"* I'd written back, lifting my left hand to show my wedding ring, figuring that would be that. I'd shifted in my seat while the stranger considered this for a moment. He was looking at the PowerPoint slides when he finally jotted a note back. *"Me, too,"* he wrote. *"So what?"*

He'd looked at me for a moment then, and the world felt very quiet, like some terrible, yellow calm before a storm. Then, casually, carefully, he'd placed his hand right up against mine so that our pinkie fingers were touching—just barely touching.

I felt my breath catch and my heart thud against my ribs, and it didn't feel like *romance* or *desire*. It felt shocking and dangerous and irresistible—like some sparking electric fence at the boundary of a forbidden property.

My wedding band had, up until then, held *Lord of the Rings*–like powers that made me invisible to other men, to second glances. But all of a sudden, the ring had failed and marriage hadn't protected me. I felt my shimmering dark insides rippling with fire, breaking me apart, burning whatever rickety bridge had been holding me together, leaving me utterly exposed as I sat there, heart beating, wanting to pull my hand away—but unable to do so.

In the conference room, there was nowhere to go, no way to escape. I was hemmed in by my coworkers and my boss and a hundred industry bigwigs, glued to the coarse fabric of my theater-style seat. There were warning flares going off in my chest one after another. *This is bad,* the lights were saying. *Danger, danger,* the lights were saying—but from this faraway distance they almost looked pretty.

They almost felt like fireworks.

After the session I'd ducked out of the room without looking back, my face burning red, my heart pounding irregularly in my throat. Even as I walked out of the building to my car and unlocked it with shaking hands, the stranger's face was already fading. He was becoming a two-dimensional stock photo, nondescript and forgettable. And yet at the same time he was changing everything.

Because, really, it wasn't about the stranger himself. It was about the way his attention made me *feel.* At first blush, truth and fiction feel exactly the same. It doesn't have to be *actual love* to make your pupils dilate, to make your adrenal glands pump chemicals into your bloodstream, to flood your body with dopamine and phenylethylamine, to quicken your breath, to make the dark void around you explode with stars.

It doesn't have to be anything, really, to make you feel alive . . . just for a second.

Imagine that you're *desperate* to feel alive.

Can you see how a moment like that might change everything?

❖

I wake up in the Bowling Green Econo Lodge the next morning of the road trip. A small slat of sunlight is knifing through the curtains. Dane and Liam are asleep on either side of me—Dane's hair swept up like a small tsunami on his head, Liam's chubby arm draped across his eyes—but I can tell by their shallow breathing that they'll be waking up soon.

I lie there and look at the dust motes floating along the ray of light and wonder why I feel so unsettled. Was there a dream? If so, I can't remember it clearly as I lie there on the hotel sheets, looking up at the popcorn ceiling. I sigh, pick up my phone to check the time, and see a text message on my screen. CAN'T WAIT TO SEE YOU! it says.

Everything clicks into place. *That's right,* I think. *I'm supposed to see Jake today. And I haven't told Andrew yet.*

The realization makes me restless and fidgety, and I throw the blankets off and walk over to the window to call Andrew. I'm waiting for him to answer the phone when Dane sits up. "Are we at Florida?" he slurs.

"No, honey. We're at the hotel, remember?"

"Oh."

"Hey, Presh!" Andrew says when he picks up the phone. He sounds happy and energetic, like a person who had a long peaceful night of sleep in his own bed.

"Hey," I answer groggily, midway through the yawn I just caught from Liam.

"Long night?"

"Kind of," I say. I look around, my vision fuzzy without my contacts. The hotel room is littered with the remnants of our evening: the cold, half-eaten pizza sitting in the soggy cardboard box on the round table; the tiny, wet swimming trunks crumpled against the wall; the straight-backed hotel chairs, still pulled in front of the TV, where Dane and Liam sat, eating pizza and watching *SpongeBob*. I look at my nightstand and sigh with relief when I see that I only managed to finish about a third of the bottle of wine before I passed out next to the kids.

"Actually, I have no idea what time we finally fell asleep." I sigh and roll my neck in an attempt to release some of the kinks from sleeping. "I thought I'd have time alone after they went to sleep at night. To write. Or watch TV. Or hear myself think. Not so much."

"Well, I could have told you that."

"Thanks a lot," I say flatly.

He laughs easily. I sigh and let go of the curtain. "Enough about my travel angst. How was *your* night?"

"Pretty good," he says, and he runs through the details of his evening at home. I picture him at the counter of our clean, quiet kitchen—the giant eighties ball fixture lighting the winter morning gray, the cupboards closed neatly instead of flung open like I usually leave them. He sounds a little lonely.

"Want to talk to the kiddos?" I ask, and then pass the phone on to Liam, who smiles at the phone and says nothing, and then Dane, who talks distractedly, eyes fixed on morning cartoons. "Ya miss me, Dad?" he asks, staring at *Curious George.*

When I get the phone back, I clear my throat. "So I might see Jake Cook at some point today," I say. I'm trying to sound casual, but I say it in one long exhale.

"Who?"

"You know," I say, peeking through the curtains. Beyond the Econo Lodge parking lot, the sun is bright against the snow-less fields. "My old high-school friend? He's the one who used to play piano for that band that came to Minnesota that once? The songwriter friend I have in Nashville?" It's unnatural and heavy-handed, the way I keep insisting on our super-casual friendship, and though Andrew answers with an equally low-key and super-cool "Okay. Yeah, I remember him," it sounds a little strained, too.

"Anyway, we might try to connect at some point. And I think

he and his wife and their small group might come to my reading tonight." I add "his wife" and "their small group" purposefully. It's a clunky subtext that I want to make sure that Andrew hears over the spotty cell connection as I stand up again, restless, and pace in front of the window. What I want Andrew to focus on here is not that I will be seeing another man but that this man is *happily married,* that he has a *small group,* that *there is nothing to worry about.*

I'm not trying to hide anything, really, but I'm trying to skirt around that inevitable long beat of silence when we both go back to the end of that summer. That almost-affair with the graphic designer who I also had sworn was "just a friend." I'm trying to make it feel casual to Andrew . . . but also, I'm trying to convince *myself.* I'm trying to drown out the sound of my failures with men even as they're banging around and around inside me like some oversize load of laundry in the machine.

"Okay," Andrew says cautiously. "Cool." And I can't see his face, so I'm not sure if it's trust or detachment at the back of his voice. Maybe a mix of both.

"And Leigh!" I add quickly. "Of course, the kids and I are staying with Leigh, and I'm super excited to see her. And I'm having dinner with Jane's niece and her family before the reading." *See all these people?* I'm trying to explain. *This is not like last time,* I'm trying to say. *He's one in a long string of acquaintances, one conversation in a day of small talk.* I'm trying to tell us both, *It'll be all right.*

"So another full day," he says, and I think that maybe he gets it. Gets *me,* even from thirteen hours and eight hundred miles away.

"Another full day." I sigh, and suddenly it seems exhausting— all those people, all those unfamiliar corners of Nashville. Our possessions, spewed all over the hotel room, needing to be picked up, packed up, hauled downstairs to the car. "I wish I were home," I say quietly.

"Yeah, but I just looked at the weather. Seventy degrees in Nashville today. *Seventy!*"

I laugh a little. "I know. *That* I'm excited about."

"Soak it up, sweets," he tells me. "It'll be awesome."

We're halfway to Nashville when I get a text message from Jake: WHEN ARE YOU GOING TO BE HERE? he wants to know. I HAVE COFFEE AT MY STUDIO!

I HAVE COFFEE WITH ME IN THE CAR, I say slowly into my phone microphone—my half-assed attempt at avoiding the death trap of texting-while-driving.

I HAVE CARIBOU COFFEE, he amends.

OH. WELL THEN. I JUST HAVE CRAPPY HOTEL COFFEE.

SEE? MINE'S WAY BETTER. HURRY UP!

I'M RUNNING A LITTLE BEHIND, I say. I PROBABLY WON'T MAKE IT BEFORE TEN OR TEN THIRTY.

BOO, Jake says. I HAVE A MEETING THEN. The emoticon he adds next to his reply is a sad face.

SORRY WE'RE SO LATE. WE HAD A LITTLE TROUBLE GETTING ON THE ROAD.

I'm understating here. The truth is that I managed to drive twenty blissful, sunny miles on I-65—arm out the window, singing loud and tunelessly along with Bob Dylan—before I realized that I'd left my computer cord plugged in by the hotel nightstand and had to go back.

THIS AFTERNOON? he tries again. I'M FREE AFTER LUNCH.

I don't answer right away. Instead I set the phone down in my lap and look out the window, considering how to respond. On the sides of the highway, tractors are rumbling slowly along the soybean fields. The men inside are ruddy and weathered and wearing scrubby old John Deere caps. I envy their slow certitude as they roll along.

The hesitancy I feel about all this has little to do with Jake and a lot to do with my complicated history with men. I am thinking, as I pass by the farmers and the semis and the cornfields, about the Guy at the Conference and the Guy at the Coffee Shop and about all the other guys over the years. The strangers to whom I have looked for some kind of validation: a nod of the head, a raised eyebrow, a half smile. A coarse compliment, a catcall, a come-on—I have wanted all of it. I have *needed* it all.

"A problem with flirting" is probably what you'd call it, but *flirting* seems to me too gentle and silly a word. It's a word that conjures crop-top-wearing teenagers at amusement parks, laughing and tickling and hair-flipping. *Flirting* is pink and cherry-flavored. It's carbonated and innocent. And whatever it is that I do, it's not that.

The version of flirting that I struggle with is darker and more subtle than all that. When my inner landscape feels dark and I can't stand to look at my own broken, mangled insides anymore, flirting lets me playact as if I'm someone else. A "cool chick." A beautiful stranger. Someone's Manic Pixie Dream Girl. And contrived as it all might be, those come-ons and pickup lines are the easiest and fastest way I know to crank down the volume on the niggling voices of self-doubt and self-loathing cawing back and forth at each other in my head. Flirting is a casino game that I can't stop playing. A Brandy Alexander straight to the brain.

If there were a support group for this kind of thing, I'd be there every week, sitting on a metal chair, clutching my Styrofoam cup of coffee, standing up to say, "I'm afraid that I don't exist if men don't notice me." And I don't think I'd be the only one in that hypothetical circle of both the happily and less-than-happily married, because in the end the compulsive drive toward this kind of flirting—much like the compulsive desire to look at Internet pornography—has little to do with your marriage and a lot to do with that smooth, addictive cocktail of excitement and desire, escape and control.

It's possible, I think, to be addicted to a certain kind of feeling. I was. I still am, because I don't think addictions ever really go away. And it's winter. Again. The faith void of silence has spread out before me again, and when everything feels this dark, the drug that I crave is this feeling: the sensation of *being seen*. I find myself craving it even now, as I drive in my minivan with my kids, surrounded by grizzled truck drivers and families in SUVs and leather-skinned motorcyclists. It hardly matters who does the noticing. All that matters is that feeling—that ninety-proof shot of desire, worth, and acceptance.

The phone buzzes again on my lap and jerks me back to the moment. THIS AFTERNOON? Jake asks again, and I realize that I never did give him an answer.

I shake the haunted memories out of my head. *Jake's just a friend,* I tell myself. But still, I can't help wondering if my insides are too broken and scabby right now for all this. If I'm too much of a junkie, if I'm too much of a mess.

Jake and I weren't particularly close in high school; there'd been a few friendly moments, but we'd really only recently connected via social media. Still, I remember clearly that he'd been something of a flirt, too. Maybe as good as me. Maybe better.

I wait one more beat before telling my phone to write, I'M THINKING OF TAKING THE KIDS TO CENTENNIAL PARK. WANT TO MEET US THERE? I have to say "Centennial Park" three times before the phone understands what I'm saying and translates it appropriately.

COOL. I'LL TRY TO STOP BY, Jake says.

Another beat. DON'T TEXT AND DRIVE, he writes, and adds a winking emoticon.

TOUCHÉ, I say, and I'm delighted when my phone understands my French. I add my own winking emoticon, stick my phone back in the cup holder, and proceed to worry about whether or not the winky face was too flirty the rest of the way to Nashville.

If the metaphor is true and there is in fact a Bible Belt strapped across the high-waisted jeans of America, Nashville might be its buckle. At the very least, it's one of the notches.

Nashville is home to more than seven hundred churches, several seminaries, three major denominational publishing arms, and a handful of Christian-music labels. The Gideons are there with their piles of hotel Bibles, as is the Gospel Music Association with its golden, dove-shaped awards.

Other than these bare but telling facts, most of what I know about the place comes from episodes of ABC's new prime-time show *Nashville*. Every Wednesday night I watch Connie Britton and Hayden Panettiere as they don sleek leather cowboy boots, sing duets with beautiful men, and let their lives spiral in and out of disaster against a musical backdrop of steel guitars and country acoustic rock.

Somewhere beyond the television glitz, Christian publishers are churning out Bibles, and twenty-one accredited colleges and universities are teaching Nietzsche. The city lights glow fluorescent—*Nashvegas!*—and foodies are adding cardamom and coconut milk to their espressos.

Nashville, it seems to me, can't get away from her roots—*doesn't really want to*—but she wants to be more than she's always been. She is an amalgamation, a paradox, a split personality.

In short, Nashville is me.

I'd spent the rest of the drive into the city cobbling together fictions about what Nashville might hold for us. I imagined myself pushing the kids through the humming heart of a cosmopolitan city in the stroller, all of us lulled by the melodies of scruffy-bearded troubadours and the warmth of the southern sun.

But by the time we arrive at Centennial Park for a picnic lunch at noon, my romantic notions about the city have evaporated.

We arrived an hour late for our morning playdate with Leigh and her nannying charge, so our outing to the neighborhood playground was rushed and a little stressful. Our trip right afterward to the city Publix for picnic stuff wasn't any better, marked by wrong turns and mounting lunch-hour traffic that made me grip the steering wheel until my hands were sweaty on the vinyl. All the while Dane and Liam chanted "We want chips!" from the backseat with a kind of frenetic determination that made me realize we were on the brink of mutiny.

Sure enough, inside the Publix my children made terrorist-level grocery demands at alarmingly loud volumes. They wanted a giant crate of raspberries. Apples in every color. Doritos. The box of Swiss Cake Rolls from an endcap. An empty muffin tin. Popsicles and Go Diego bubble bath and sugarcoated gummy worms and a ham. By the time we were in the checkout lane, I had stooped to negotiations whispered through clenched teeth. *"I'll buy you these finger-clip laser lights if you sit in the cart. I'll buy you these Easter-chick stickers if you stop screaming RIGHT NOW."*

Outside, in the parking lot, Liam scrambled out of my arms and took off, weaving drunkenly between parking spots and moving cars, and I had to chase him down, yelling, while around me Nashville natives looked on with a mixture of pity and disdain. By the time I'd strapped the boys into their car seats, they were both crying. I sat in the front seat, the door propped open, my hands shaking with fury and exhaustion, not even noticing the warmth on the back of my neck as I tried to spread peanut butter onto slices of bread with a flimsy plastic knife.

By the time I navigated the van into an iffy parking spot on the street outside Centennial Park (*Is this a legal parking spot? Am I going to get a ticket? You know what, I don't even care*), I was on the verge of tears myself. And by the time I got a text from Jake saying he was there at the park and where were we anyway, I was vulnerable and frazzled and wanting a drink—of what, I didn't much care. Wine? Tequila? Flirty bantering with an old high-school acquaintance who I assured my husband was "just a friend, just a friend, just a friend"?

I can see Jake before I can hear him, walking across the sprawl of manicured lawn around Nashville's famous replica of the Parthenon. I read somewhere that this copycat structure was built to the exact same dimensions as the one in Athens. It was built in 1897 as a temporary structure for the Tennessee Centennial and International Exposition, but when the expo was over, no one could bear to tear it down. It had become a touchstone, a tribute to higher education and culture and all the ways Nashville was rebuilding itself in those post–Civil War years: the Athens of the South.

Jake is older now, with a drastically receding hairline, but I recognize him immediately—even from a dozen yards away. I lift my hand and wave, and when he smiles and waves back, I can still see traces of the seventeen-year-old Jake that I knew—the show-choir star, the self-assured songwriter, the kid who produced his own album of earnest faith-filled songs and sold copies in the choir room between classes. Once, before he left for college, we sat on a bench by a lake and talked about going out into the *secular world* and *making a difference for Jesus*. I can see us so clearly at this moment—young and full of hope and certainty, arrows pointed straight toward the future that we'd imagined for ourselves, lit up Nashvegas style for Jesus.

"Hi!" I say when he gets close enough to hear me. I stand up from my spot at our picnic table, where I've been sitting alone, surrounded by the discarded detritus of our lunch. Sandwiches with one or two bites taken out of them. Half-eaten bags of Aldi-brand barbecue chips. Juice boxes. Dane and Liam have scampered a few feet away from the picnic table by now, abandoning their meal for the freedom of the wide-open spaces.

"Well, hey!" he says, and he reaches forward to give me an awkward side hug.

"Good to see you," I say, ending the hug with a polite back pat and putting my sunglasses on so that I can see him through the glare of the afternoon. "Thanks for coming!"

"You look . . ." He pauses and looks at me, and I'm not sure what I want in this moment.

I've been ground down by the last thousand miles of highway and the trip to Publix, and right now I feel like nothing so much as a ragged, stained, irrelevant *mom*. I'd give almost anything in this moment to have someone look at me like I'm not. After all, I'm an addict, a junkie. And if this old high-school friend were to say something slightly flirtatious under the golden light of Nashville, I might find myself angling myself toward it, letting it in.

Jake looks at me. I look at him.

"Tired," Jake says at last. "Girl, you look *tired*."

I exhale and laugh, and it feels like a kind of pass over, an act of grace, a small salvation. I have been passed over by the lightning that might ignite me for one brief moment before burning me to the ground. Before destroying everything. I breathe a silent prayer of thanks and then smirk at Jake. "Thanks a lot," I say dryly.

"Seriously. Did you even sleep last night?"

I laugh again, and just like that—it's gone. It's a sudden change in weather. The clouds clear, and I can see my *friend*. Jake. He is no longer the flirty older boy he used to be in high school, the one who sometimes used to wink at me in the hall. And it turns out that I'm no longer the girl at that technical writing conference, so filled with the dead kindling of a dried-up faith that she could burst into flames at any moment.

I am relieved. And I know that I'm not all the way healed. That this angling, this thirst, this drive to flirt my way toward *feeling something* will likely be a lifelong struggle. But also—I'm not as shattered as I used to be either. I hadn't known that before, and it gives me a boost of hope. All this time I've been getting stronger. I hadn't noticed it, but it had happened anyway.

I look at Jake, and I can see myself reflected in his sunglasses—pale in my pink shirt and faded in my blue jeans, uncertain, and yes, *tired*. He looks a little tired, too, in his fitted jacket and skinny jeans, a few wispy strands of hair hanging on resolutely to the top of his head. We have come so far to stand here, at the edge of the fake Parthenon, keeping a healthy distance between us as the sun begins its slow afternoon descent.

I point toward the kids, who are ten feet away, running circles around a small landscaping boulder, climbing on top and then spreading their arms wide, jumping off. "You'd be tired, too," I say. Dane and Liam's abandoned peanut-butter sandwiches are getting crusty in the sun.

"Wow," he says. Jake and his wife don't have kids yet, and I don't know how to explain what the last two hours have been like to a person who has not yet experienced it firsthand. So I just nod and say, "Yup."

"Are they always like that?"

"Pretty much."

"Huh."

"Come on," I say. "You have time for a quick walk?"

Jake looks at his watch. "A really short one. I have to get back to work."

"Got it." I shove the uneaten lunch into the basket underneath the stroller and call the kids, and we walk toward the small man-made pond in front of the Parthenon. Dane and Liam run ahead, and I yell things like "Red light!" And "Wait for Mama!" And "I'm SERIOUS. Wait for Mom or we're leaving RIGHT NOW." Jake looks at me side-eyed, like he's not sure what to make of my Serious Mom Voice. "They won't pay any attention," I tell him. "But at least if I do this, people know I'm trying."

He laughs a little, and I ask him about his work—producing albums for upcoming artists. He talks, and I'm listening, but his words are slightly muted in my ears as I watch the boys sprinting ahead, the sun resting on the tops of their heads. They stop every few feet and peer into the pond, both of them bending over, their elastic blue jeans riding low. For a moment I feel so oddly split between past and present, between the girl I was fifteen years ago and the woman I am now.

Jake is walking beside me, so clearly a figment of a past life. Next to him I feel like a memory of myself—that rail of a girl with her WWJD bracelet and all her hope. That girl who knew exactly what it meant when she said, "I have a relationship with Jesus Christ."

We walk to the far end of the pond, where a boat is settled in the murky water and two park employees are pulling up the bloated, floating bodies of dead fish with nets. Dane shouts and waves. "Hey! Hey! Hey, mister! Can I see the fish!" The men oblige him with good-natured smiles, lifting their nets so that he can see the motionless silver scales catch the light. "Cool," he says.

"Cool," Liam repeats reverently.

Jake looks at his watch, and I can tell he's had about all he can take of the under-four crowd. "Need to get going?" I ask.

"Yeah." He looks at me and shifts a little. "Listen, I know I said that Alicia and I were going to try to make it to your book reading tonight . . . but we're not going to be able to."

"Oh," I say, waving my hand like it's no big deal. "I get it. It's fine."

"No, it's not. I really wanted to be there, but our small group from church is having kind of a crisis, and we need to be there."

"Don't worry about it," I tell him. "It's a college reading. In a library. It's probably going to be awkward."

"I really wish we could be there. I want you to meet Alicia."

"I know. I do, too," I tell him. "But really, it's fine."

We say good-bye, and Jake gives me one more side hug and waves before heading off across the lawn. I look at the boys kneeling at the side of the pond, picking up stones, and then I look back, and he has vanished behind the Parthenon's columns, beyond the college boys throwing Frisbees and the hopefuls strumming their guitars and the long-legged girls tanning in the grass. He is gone, and if this were a Christian romance novel, this would be the part where my "victory over the flesh" was rewarded by an instant rush of palpable God love.

But that's not what happens. Instead I feel suddenly lost—as if a part of myself is disappearing all over again: the girl who wanted to be a Bright Light for Jesus; the passionate one who felt so much like a lit firecracker, ready to explode into the future.

For a few minutes, I'd remembered her so clearly. I'd felt the thrown light of her naïve hope bouncing across the years, and it had been enough to remind me what I had once been before I stopped being able to *feel it*. But now the empty numbness inside of me feels so big that it's a country, a universe, a black hole sucking me in. When I bend down next to Dane and Liam by the pond, I feel it there, rippling over me like the small brown waves that obscure my reflection. It follows me as I push them in our creaky, garage-sale double stroller along the paved path of Centennial Park and leans against me as I stand at the side of the playground under an old tree. Nashville moms stand in pods of fitted jackets and highlighted curly hair, watching their kids, drinking coffee out of paper cups, laughing.

There's a story in the Bible, in the book of Exodus: Moses is working to free the Israelites from their slave masters, and God brings a plague of darkness on the Egyptians. *Stretch out your hand toward the sky so that darkness spreads over Egypt,* he tells Moses in that annoyingly clear way that he *tells* Moses things. *Darkness that can be felt.* This is what God had rained down upon the Egyptians when they'd refused to let his people go. This is what it feels like now as I stand in the center of Nashville, and I can't figure out why. What could I have done to deserve darkness like a plague, like a disease, like a haunting? Have I failed in my faith journey in some terrible way? Have I brought it on myself, like Pharaoh, this *darkness that can be felt*?

I think about Andrew at home. Why didn't I push harder for him to come? If I'd pushed it, he probably would have. He would've rescheduled interviews, taken days off, made it work. But the truth is, I hadn't wanted him to. I'd wanted to do this by myself. I'd thought I was on a pilgrimage of some kind, thought

I was going to find God, find myself, find *something* besides ghost stories, besides the same old stuff that I thought I'd left behind.

The next few hours pass in an unfamiliar blur of new streets and rush-hour traffic. At the apartment of my friend's niece, we eat Domino's pizza and drink homemade lemonade and sit on the deck overlooking the trees. Afterward we drive to the near-empty library of a local Christian university for my book reading and arrive embarrassingly late.

I hurry, out of breath and frustrated, to the front of the vast, quiet room. I stand at the podium to the left of wide, tall windows pressed with the broad back of the nighttime, and I read the story of my faith journey in bits and pieces to the sparse group—twelve women, one man. The librarian's husband has taken my children to some room somewhere to play, and I feel anxious about it, anxious about the way my voice clangs around the silent, vaulted places, anxious about the book in my hands that feels, tonight, like some kind of fossil—as if whatever was alive and vital at the heart of my faith has disappeared, leaving only an imprint.

I talk about my evangelical Christian upbringing as if it's in the past, as if my faith is about to burst into something new and better. I answer questions as if I know the answers. And when I wrap up the reading, it feels like a kind of fiction to close the book—as if the story can actually be wrapped up so neatly. As if I've figured anything out.

That night it takes nearly an hour to get back to Leigh's house from the reading and another hour to get the boys wound down and settled onto the air mattress on the floor of her office. When they finally quiet, Leigh hands me a mug brownie, a glass of wine, and a White Sox blanket. I sit on her couch and promptly burst into tears.

"I'm sorry," I keep saying, pawing at my eyes.

"Don't worry about it," she says. "Go ahead and cry." She hands me a tissue, and even though she's an Internet friend whom I've met only once in real life, I believe her. I put down my mug brownie and sob into my hands for no reason I can understand, except that I'm so tired, so far from any kind of resolution, so far from God and the girl who used to know and love him so desperately. I ramble through snotty hands about the kids and the road and the reading and tomorrow's drive to Atlanta.

"I don't know why I thought this was such a good idea," I say when I've calmed down enough to get a coherent sentence out. "'Let's drive a hundred thousand miles to Florida, kids! It'll be fun!' I'm an idiot."

And I'm talking about the road, but what I'm actually trying to say is that, it's *seventy degrees and sunny* . . . but the darkness that I'm working so hard to flee is still here. I'm beginning to wonder if it's actually *in me*. If it's been in me all this time.

"You're not an idiot. And you'll be okay, you know," Leigh says, pulling her own White Sox blanket tighter over her legs and handing me back my mug brownie.

"You think?"

She nods, and I get the feeling that she's not just talking about the road trip.

"I *know*," she says, and smiles at me. "Now, eat your brownie. I made it from scratch. *In the microwave.* I mean, *gourmet*."

Nashville, Tennessee, to Fayetteville, Georgia

Wednesday, February 19, 2014

"*Morning time, Mom.*"

I groan and pry my eyes open in the slant of light coming through the bedroom blinds. Liam is bent over me, his nose grazing mine, all blue eyes and mussed morning hair and expectancy.

I blink a couple of times and rub at my eyes, grab for my phone on the bookshelf next to me and look blearily at the time: *six thirty in the morning.* "Up!" Liam says. "Up, Mom."

I spent the night smushed between Dane and Liam on the slowly deflating double air mattress in Leigh's office. Sometime during the night, a depression formed beneath me, and now I'm sunk almost all the way to the floor. Also, sometime during the night Dane rolled on top of my right arm. He's now shifting into wakefulness as I try to carefully extract myself from under his bony back. My arm is numb and pin-prickled with pain. *Morning time.*

In the dim early-morning light of Leigh's apartment, I try to persuade the kids to quietly watch *Lego Ninjago* on Netflix so that they don't wake our hostess while I begin to gather our things and get ready. Today is another full day of driving, and I'd like to be on the road as quickly and with as little drama as possible. But when I come out of the bathroom after getting clothes and makeup on, they're deep into a kicking fight over who has more room on the couch. When Leigh shuffles out of her room a few minutes later looking half asleep, I trip over myself apologizing for the noise and the chaos that we've brought into her morning routine. She waves it off graciously, but by the time I've buckled the kids into their seats and hugged her good-bye, I can tell she's just about as frazzled as I am.

"There's a great little bagel shop just near here if you want to grab some coffee or breakfast," she says, looping her purse around her arm. Her sunglasses are perched on top of her cute pixie cut, and she points just down the road to a jumble of trendy shops bunched up along the road.

"Thanks. Maybe I will," I say, though I know I won't. What I will *actually* do is get us out of Nashville proper as quickly as possible. On the fringes of town, where the traffic has slowed and stretched out, I'll stop, finally, to refuel the van. Then, and only then, will I haul Dane and Liam inside. At that nondescript gas station in the middle of the sprawling nowhere, I'll let them choose a doughnut while I fill a paper cup with cheap coffee from the canisters near the candy bars.

I have gotten used to cobbling together meals from between postcard displays—muffins and fruit cups and, if we're lucky, yogurt packaged in plastic tubes. I've gotten adept at explaining to

Dane why we can't buy a Tennessee-shaped key chain or a cowboy hat or whatever other gas-station kitsch he's set his eye on. From buzzing glass-door refrigerators, I'll find cartons of milk between the Powerade and the energy drinks and the Pepsi products, and then I'll stand behind wizened truck drivers buying packs of cigarettes, waiting to pay for our assortment of prepackaged goodies.

In my Dream Road Trip, I'm getting to know the feel and topography and unique character of every state and town we pass, but in real life one day is not enough time to get any true sense of a place. My experiences of each place are thin and lifeless, not even beginning to scratch the surface. I've seen only one tiny, suburban strip of Indy and the rain-slicked back of Louisville. All I know of Nashville is a fake Parthenon and bad rush-hour traffic. I don't know the taste of the best pancakes or the best burger in any of these cities. I didn't really get a chance to experience the textures of small-town streets, the rhythm of downtown Indy under my feet.

What I *am* getting a sense of, though, is the nature of the *road*. I'm beginning to understand that highways and interstates all have their own rhythms, their own rituals and sounds and tastes and songs. The cities where we stay change every day, sometimes more than once, but the road strings us together and gives me a sense of bearing. I'm learning the gravelly hum of wheels against asphalt. I'm breathing in the road itself: the exhaust of semis mixed with the dense smell of soil and water from the living fields around us.

When I open the windows and put my hand out, I can feel the particular air of the interstate press against my skin with a kind of relentless force. BPs and Mobils and SuperAmericas with their packaged food and colorful endcaps and bins of boxed candy—they have become my touchstones over the last several days. I've begun to crave the distinct aroma of gas-station coffee, hot from paper cups with flimsy plastic lids: CAUTION: HOT. It's beginning to taste like home.

The road out of Nashville slows and sputters for a while with the morning commuters, and then silently it slips out of town and into the consistent anonymity of the interstate system. I-24 slants east, alongside towering bluffs and sheer drops, all of it dipped in sunshine.

A few hours later, just outside Chattanooga, we slam to a sudden stop when traffic inexplicably jams up. We're ten feet from the last exit, and I follow suit with a couple others, reversing slowly and cautiously along the shoulder until we're back at the gravelly edge of the exit ramp and can make an escape.

I sigh and pull into a strip-mall parking lot, where the kids instantly recognize the Dollar Tree sign and beg to go inside and buy something. These are things I did not expect on my Epic Winter Road Trip: detours and deviations and strip-mall dollar stores. Darkness trailing behind like some somber specter. In the Dollar Tree, Dane and Liam examine the chintzy toys while I stand in the aisle next to cheap island-themed decor—pink plastic cocktail classes and paper umbrellas and plastic leis—and map out a new route to Georgia.

The detour I find weaves us out of the parking lot and through the back roads of Chattanooga, where the two-lane road sidles up to stony ridges and the broad backs of small, stout mountains. We're so close that I can see the texture of the rock and the way rivulets of water cascade into puddles at the bases. I drive with my windows down, my arm draped over the side of the car. The whole town smells like funnel cake: sugar and summertime and cooking oil, and by the time we make it back to I-75, I'm feeling a little less broken.

We arrive in Fayetteville just as the sun is beginning to set over Georgia. My cousin's house is at the end of a sprawling subdivision where every house has acreage. It takes me a few minutes to pair the address on my phone with the ranch-style house surrounded by big trees, but when I do, we coast up the gravel driveway and park under the pecan trees. An old golden retriever with white fur around his eyes wags his tail and nuzzles our hands while we tumble out of the van and climb the wooden steps to the back patio door.

A small blond girl, maybe eight years old, flings the door open and stares at us a minute or two before her mom, my cousin Audrey, appears behind her. "Come in, come in!" she says. "Joanna, say hello!"

Inside, Audrey gives me a hug. She's as pencil-thin as she was at age twelve when we spent our summers at TaHaZouka Park in our grandparents' Nebraska town, researching flirting techniques with uninterested preteen boys and recording our findings methodically in a small blue notebook. Even her haircut is the same—long and light. But her arms look strong and her eyes look wise and a little tired, and four little girls jump around her and call her "Mama." It's the first time I've seen her in more than a decade.

On the vaulted white walls of Audrey's wide, windowed living room, she has dozens of framed black-and-white photos of her four daughters—all with white-blond hair, all at different ages, all grinning and dimpled. Around the corner a door opens to an attic playroom that has a ramp and a rope instead of stairs, and my kids look at it for one wide-eyed moment before they grip the rope and begin to climb. "This is kind of awesome," I say to her as we lean on the door frame and watch them scurry up the unfinished wood.

"It's pretty much a safety hazard." She shrugs. "We meant to make it into a slide, but it's too steep. This actually seemed safer—if you can believe it."

"Watch me, Mom!" Dane says as he scales the ramp and stands barefoot and toothy at the top, grinning in triumph.

"Awesome!" I reply, cringing a little when Liam follows his brother up, clumsy and confident and not about to be left out.

Liam—who had three sets of stitches in various spots on his head before age two—climbs deliberately, his short legs moving resolutely up the ramp until he, too, makes it to the top, sighs happily, and wanders out of sight.

"You're insane," I tell my cousin.

"I know," Audrey says. "We had a really hard time explaining it to the social-services people," she tells me. Audrey and her husband are in the middle of trying to adopt two boys from the foster system, and I can imagine a county employee gaping up at the rough-hewn wood of the playroom's ramp of terror.

I laugh. "I bet you did."

"They're good up there. Let's sit down. Want something to drink?" I follow her to her farmhouse kitchen, where she clanks around in her cabinets, getting glasses for ice water. "Where did you say you guys spent the day? Covington?"

"Yep," I said, accepting the glass of water from her. "Thanks."

"Don't take this the wrong way . . . but *Covington*?" She leads us back to the living room, where she sits down on the couch. *"Why?"*

I laugh, because it *is* a little absurd. Instead of heading straight into the Atlanta metropolis, where I could have taken the kids to the World of Coca-Cola or the Georgia Aquarium or to Olympic Park, I'd curved around it. I'd gone an extra thirty-five miles southeast to Covington, a town of 13,452.

"The short answer is that I had a meet-up with some blog readers there," I tell her. I explain, briefly, that before my trip I'd thrown a vague invitation out into the pixilated world of my blog, proposing a handful of informal hangouts along our trip route: *I'd love to meet you,* I'd told my readers. *E-mail if you're interested!* And the e-mails came. And so did the people, showing up at every place we stopped. Not by the hundreds, but one by one, saying hello, telling me their names, making me feel a little less alone every time.

"Okay," she says. "Cool. And the long answer?"

I sigh. "Because I'm a closeted *Vampire Diaries* fan. And that's where they film it."

Audrey looks at me blankly.

"You've never heard of it, have you?" I deduce, and she shakes her head, leaving me with the somewhat embarrassing task of explaining the convoluted CW show.

The basic plot of *The Vampire Diaries* is simple: Two vampire brothers move back to their hometown of Mystic Falls. Drama ensues. Said drama is always *epic* and is usually a matter of life and death. There is a werewolf on the loose, a rogue Original Vampire with extra powers and a vendetta, a gorgeous ex-vampire girlfriend with a grudge. The parties are wilder, the make-out sessions more intense, and the heartaches more agonizing when you're a creature of the supernatural world, apparently. Life is frenetic and pulsing, like the blood pumping through the necks of would-be victims (or lovers . . . or both) all over town. It's sexy and salacious—while still being clean enough for network television—and it's aimed at teenagers, themselves dripping with hormones and desire.

While I'm explaining this, Audrey nods and sips her water, but the expression on her face is a poorly disguised mix of pity and horror. For the first time, I look around and notice that there's not even a television in the living room, which makes sense now that I think about it. Audrey was something of a prodigy, as I recall, going off to college when she should still have been in high school and then eventually going to medical school, too. Now, she home-schools her four daughters, takes classes to finish her degree, and is well down the road to adoption. Normally on winter Wednesday nights, the family goes to church for Awana clubs, where her children sing the Bible songs of our youth and trade memorized Bible verses for small jewels to pin into plastic crowns.

Where my faith crises made me reckless and cynical, hers—whatever they've been—seem to have made her surer, stronger, and more grounded. She is spreading roots deep into parts of the Christian culture that I have left behind. On their walls, framed Bible verses. On her lips, the old familiar language of my childhood faith. I have a feeling that while I'm watching *The Vampire Diaries* with a big bowl of cheese puffs, she's probably helping her children memorize Scripture and learn long division.

"I know. It's a totally dumb show. For preteens. But I just can't seem to quit it." Over the years the plot of *The Vampire Diaries* has gotten more convoluted and silly. Turns out there is nothing compelling about normalcy in the world of teen television, and the show's creators have to keep upping the ante. *The Vampire Diaries* only works if it is constantly swinging on the pendulum of life and death, if the plot keeps twisting away from a resolution. So the writers invent new dramas, create villains where the old ones have been killed off, and open the doors of magical prison worlds and let out those we thought had gone. "I keep trying, and it keeps sucking me back in like a tractor beam." I try to make the tractor beam noise. Andrew is a master of it, but when I try, it comes out like a weird gurgle, and Audrey looks at me like I've maybe been on the road too long.

"Well, was it cool? The filming? Did you see any . . . vampires?" The serious politeness with which she asks this question makes me laugh.

"No! Not a single one!" After the meet-up I'd followed a blog reader's husband across the street to Covington Square. I stood for a long time with a row of onlookers—mostly middle-aged women—squinting toward the alley next to the Mystic Grill, where a scene was purportedly being filmed *right that minute*. I'd of course harbored a secret fantasy that Ian Somerhalder—the chiseled, dreamy-eyed actor who plays the older vampire brother—might have, upon seeing me, come running out of the alley. *Addie Zierman? Is that you? I've read your book and it CHANGED MY LIFE. Can I take you out to dinner and pick your brain about faith and writing? And also, by the way, YOU LOOK GORGEOUS!* But I never even saw him. The blog reader's husband had pointed to a barely visible man tucked into the alleyway—"That's Stephan," he'd said, referring to the younger vampire brother. "You can tell because he always keeps his script in his back pocket." I'd nodded, but all I could see were the big white screens propped on metal stands, boom mikes and orange cones, and a lot of heavyset men in baseball caps with cameras. It had been epically un-epic.

"Well, that's too bad. . . ." Audrey trails off, not really knowing what else to say about the whole thing.

I wave my hand. "It's all right. It was actually kind of a fun little town. The Internet people were so kind to us, and the kids had a good time running around Covington Square. It was fine." I take a long drink of my water. "Anyway, enough vampires. What's new with *you* guys?"

From there our conversation takes a turn into more grown-up territory. Audrey talks about the recent missionary work she's done, about homeschooling her girls, about helping out at their church's Awana program, about the two foster boys they're getting ready to adopt. Her life feels as foreign to me as my *Vampire Diaries* habit must feel to her. I fold my legs underneath me on the couch and do my best to shove aside my behemoth baggage around words like *missionary* and *homeschooling* and *Awana program.*

I focus instead on the bright blue eyes that belong to my thin, strong cousin. I listen to the clomping of the kids in the playroom above. I know that these differences can, and in some ways do, separate us. They are Big Life Things that so often pit us against one another. *Mommy Wars* and *Culture Wars.* Battles and brouhahas that always seem to leave both sides bloodied and broken. They are the things that hook into my deepest insecurities about my own wobbly faith and inconsistent parenting and make me behave like the worst version of myself.

But outside the window the sun is setting pink and there are the tiniest paint dabs of light on the Georgia trees, and I find that if I stay right here in this moment, I feel none of the angst—only gratitude and hospitality, humility and love. We are in transit. We are weary travelers, and they are taking us in. This is the only thing about faith that seems to matter just now.

In the idyllic Georgia home, with its backyard playhouse and chicken coop and attic rope ramp, my cousin feeds us hot pizza and salad and pours milk into plastic tumblers for my kids. She's changed the sheets on her oldest daughter's full-size bed and handed me a pile of freshly washed blankets to make a bed on the floor for the boys. Her girls, she tells me, all prefer to sleep in the same room, on two parallel sets of bunk beds. I peek into their bedroom and see all four of them—pink-spotted pajama bottoms, mouths smelling of mint, smiles bright. Two of them are in the same bed, snuggled into a bottom bunk, whispering softly.

Back in our bedroom, Dane and Liam are fighting over who gets which pillow, and I'm whisper-shouting at them to *"Stop fighting! It doesn't matter! Both pillows are the same!"* Defeated, Dane begs to take my iPhone into the bathroom, and because "number two" has been a bit of an issue in all these unfamiliar places, I let him. The distraction might be what he needs to clear out his system. So I send him into the bathroom with the PBS app opened up and *Caillou* playing. "Be careful," I tell him.

"I *know*, Mom," he says irritably, and then he shuts the bathroom door.

❖

I've got Liam's diaper halfway on when I hear Dane start screaming in the bathroom. "Help, Mom!"

"Just a sec!" I shout, trying to secure the Velcro as Liam wiggles and dances. "Liam, stop moving," I say. He just laughs.

Dane keeps crying, but I've gotten so used to his angry, tired, four-year-old tantrums that I don't worry too much about it. "I'm coming, buddy!" I say again while I try to tug the cotton pajama bottoms over Liam's chunky legs.

"IT FELL IN!" I hear him yell.

It takes a second to register exactly what he's saying. *It fell in.* I tug the pajamas a little more, then freeze. *Nooooooo.*

I'm to the Jack-and-Jill bathroom between Audrey's kids' bedrooms in two seconds flat, but it's already too late. There it is, at the bottom of the porcelain bowl. My iPhone.

Sitting on a bed of poop.

I reach in with one swift motion and pull it out, hold it dripping over the toilet.

I snap off the case. It's meant to be "LifeProof," but the case is old and frayed in places, and I long ago lost the plug piece that covers the headphone port that makes the phone impenetrable to water. When the case is off, I scrub frantically at the naked phone with the nearest bathroom hand towel, but I know that it's too late. I can scrub all I want, but something tells me that there will be no resurrecting the poop phone.

"It was an *accident*," Dane sobs.

"I know it was," I say. I know that Dane needs to be reassured and hugged, but I can't keep the edge out of my voice as I try the power button—and nothing happens. "It's okay," I murmur unconvincingly while I shake the phone. Water drips steadily out of the headphone port. *No, no, nooooo.*

"I'm *sorry*, Mom," Dane wails.

"It's okay," I say again, even though it feels so *un*-okay that I want to scream. "Wash your hands."

I carry the phone to the kitchen as if it's a wounded bird and report the situation to Audrey, who immediately begins scouring her cabinets for rice. The rolled-up bag she finally finds has barely a quarter cup left. *Not enough.* I thank her anyway and dump the paltry remains of brown rice over my phone.

Over the low, stainless-steel kitchen sink, I scrub at the useless case with dish soap while Audrey's oldest daughter stands next to me.

"It fell in the *toilet*?" she asks, wide-eyed. "In, like, actual poop?"

Hattie, their three-year-old, runs in circles laughing. "Poop? POOP?! Poop! Poop! Poop!"

"Girls," Audrey says, giving them a warning look. Joanna smacks her lips together but continues to stare at the phone.

"In actual poop," I whisper to her. I try to smile, to see it as an eight-year-old might—*hilarious*—but it feels a little thin. I keep thinking of all that is lost in that phone, all the ways I've relied on it during this trip. It is my map, my clock, my weather forecaster. My link to the world behind me and the one ahead of me. It is the antidote to loneliness or to silence or to boredom. When the kids are sobbing and the road feels too long, all I have to do is snap a photo and it stops feeling like the end of the living world and instead begins to feel like a memory fragment—the thing that we'll laugh about later, the thing that is making me strong.

I've downloaded most of the pictures from the trip so far—but not all of them. Gone are the photos I snapped of the road spiraling through the mountains as we drove from Tennessee to Georgia. *It's so beautiful,* I thought as I watched the hills drop and the whole landscape glitter in the morning light. I held up the phone to the window for miles, snapping pictures through my finger-smudged window, trying to capture the world around me, to fix it in my mind. But those photos are gone now, along with the ones from the Covington town square that I'd taken surreptitiously while watching *The Vampire Diaries,* even though the Shusher had been adamant about *no taking photos.* I'd taken a selfie in front of the show's main hangout joint, the Mystic Grill—but that's gone now, along with the pictures I snapped of my kids, arms full of sticks and leaves, grinning madly in front of that sprawling old tree in Covington Square. All of it is lost in the drowned heart of my iPhone.

I feel a little numb as I climb down onto the sleeping bag where Dane and Liam are lying side by side. Dane is still upset, and I run my hand over the top of his hair, still a little damp and sweaty from climbing up and down the ladder into the attic playroom. "It's okay about the phone," I tell him. "Mom's not mad."

"Yes you are," he says.

"I'm just frustrated. And sad because phones cost a lot of money," I tell him, trying to figure out when our last cell-phone upgrade was—if we'll get any grace whatsoever with the soulless people at AT&T. "But I'm not mad at you. Accidents happen."

"I was just putting it on the seat so I could wash my hands," he says softly. "I didn't know it would fall in."

"I know."

I lie there for a while next to him, rubbing soft circles between his shoulder blades. *Back tickles,* Andrew calls them. "Thanks, Mom," Dane says softly, and I'm not really mad. I'm just tired. I'm just so tired.

I kiss Dane's cheek, then Liam's. "Love you, Mom." Dane sighs, he presses his palm against my cheek, his eyes heavy as he stares tenderly into mine.

"I love *you,* buddy," I whisper, and I feel buried to my neck in the bad-mom moments of the day. Particularly the ones related to the phone. The guilt piles on top of me like a kind of wet, deep sand, and I feel my eyes well up when I repeat, "I love you so much."

"Yeah." He sighs again and smiles. "I know. Can I have water?"

"Me, too!" Liam adds.

"Yeah. I'll go get some."

I bring them water. I tell them not to talk, and when they do anyway, I let it go. I put on my sweatpants, take out my contacts, throw my hair into a sloppy ponytail, and step blinking into the bright kitchen, where Audrey is cleaning up.

"You okay?" she asks as I sit down heavily at their kitchen counter.

"Meh," I grunt.

Audrey looks at me sympathetically, and her tall, kind-eyed engineer husband, Matt, goes down to the basement to bring up a bottle of sweet Georgia wine. The bottle is dusty. I can tell that an evening glass of wine is not part of their daily routine, that this is a gift, a kindness, an invitation to take what I need. They are doing what they can, serving me a mason jar filled with grace. I take it gratefully, but it goes down the wrong way, burning and choking me, and I have to run to the bathroom and hack over the sink for a while.

"Mom! What are you doing?!" Dane yells from his sleeping bag.

"I'm fine," I cough. "Go back to sleep."

I look up at my mottled reflection in the mirror, and it feels like *too much, too much, too much.* Tears burn in my eyes, and I feel dumb to cry, because it's just a *phone.* This is not a big deal. I glare at the mirror, angry with myself for being so upset, for not being able to roll with the small trials of everyday life—the problems, the inconveniences, the icy Minneapolis roads, the dark winter mornings.

For a moment at the sink, I regret all of it. The trip, the driving, the interstates. My own stupid spontaneity. *This is a First World adventure,* I think. *And I am not brave at all.*

Back in the living room, my cousin and her husband are sitting on the couch watching me with marked concern as I come back in and sit cross-legged on the love seat. "You okay?" Audrey asks softly, and that's all it takes to uncork the stopper that's been holding back the tears. All of a sudden I'm sobbing and swearing and wiping snot on my Northwestern College sweatshirt sleeve. This crying-at-people's-houses thing is getting to be an embarrassing pattern.

Audrey and Matt are Awana parents, homeschool parents,

theologically *together,* faithful in their own spiritual journeys in ways that I have not been able to be. They are not the kind of people who swear. I know this, but I can't seem to stop sobbing and babbling and saying the word *damn.*

But if they judge me for my childish tantrum and my adolescent cursing, they don't say so, don't let on even a little. Instead Matt stands up to go look for an old iPhone that I can use for the rest of the trip. "I think I have one in my office," he says.

"You don't have to do that. I'm sure I can find a cell-phone store somewhere and buy a new one."

"Don't worry about it," he says. "You can deal with all that when you get home. No reason to worry about it now if you don't have to. Let me go see if I can find it."

Audrey taps my shoulder lightly and hands me her phone. "Call your husband. You'll feel better."

"Ugh. I hope he's not mad."

"He won't be," she says. Then she smiles gently and follows Matt out of the room to give me privacy. I thank her, dial the phone, and scrub at my eyes while it rings.

"So my phone's dead," I say as soon as Andrew picks up the unidentified Georgia phone number that I've called him from.

"I wondered," he says, but he doesn't sound upset, only concerned. "What happened? You okay?"

"Dane dropped it. Into a toilet full of poop."

Andrew's laugh comes unexpected and hearty over the phone lines, and I find myself laughing a little, too—a drowned, wry, hiccupping giggle that slips out in spite of myself.

"Noooo! Sweetie!" He says the "sweetie" part tenderly, and I'm grateful for his familiar voice, his deep understanding, the way I can almost see him there in our kitchen, sitting on a stool in his green plaid pajama pants, his eyes crinkling as he laughs.

"I guess shit happens," I say weakly.

Andrew laughs harder. "Sometimes the shit hits the fan," he says. "And sometimes your phone hits the shit."

Outside, the night is star-spangled, coming bright through the windows as I hold the borrowed phone close and listen to my husband's voice near and far all at once.

"I'm so dumb," I say.

"No."

"I shouldn't have let him take it to the bathroom."

"You were trying to help."

"Why do these things always happen to me?" In my mind I tally the expensive things I've lost or ruined or broken over the years. The phone I dropped into the snowbank outside the corporate offices where I worked and that I couldn't find for a whole week. The phone I had after that, which Dane dropped into the water table with the frogs. The camera I left out in the rainstorm and the one I dropped on the pavement in Duluth.

A few weeks before this trip, I spilled a cup of coffee on my Mac, and I'm still half waiting for it to give up and die. Even the van I'm driving has my mark on it—its bumper hanging off from where I rear-ended those teenage boys last year. "Seriously. I'm a liability. You should make me use one of those giant, indestructible eighties cell phones—like that one Zack has on *Saved by the Bell.*

He laughs again. "It'll all work out."

"It will?"

"It will. Now, tell me about the Vamps."

I sniffle, laugh, and tell him about Covington, where middle-aged women are probably still lined up along the curb, waiting. Where I imagine that the actors are just leaving now. Checking their watches, stretching their tired arms, heading for home—or some version of it—to rest from another weary, average day.

FAYETTEVILLE, GEORGIA, TO ORMOND BEACH, FLORIDA

Thursday, February 20, 2014

The trip from Fayetteville, Georgia, to Ormond Beach, Florida, is supposed to take six hours and thirteen minutes, but I realize as soon as the green mileage signs begin flashing that it will take us *so much longer*. It's our fourth consecutive day of long drives, and the kids are *over it*. I have to stop at gas stations twice before lunch for potty and snack breaks. Kid Time has become a yawning chasm spreading farther and farther across the day, and I'm about to fling myself off of it.

Outside the car the weather is getting warmer and warmer. "Eighty degrees today!" Audrey had said before I left this morning.

"Naturally," I'd whined, petulant, as I waited for Matt's old phone to reload with my contacts and apps. "Because we have to be in the car *all day long* instead of lying on the beach and enjoying it!"

Now I roll down the window and try to feel every last one of those eighty degrees of warmth with the tips of my fingers, but the kids complain that they can't hear the movie, so it goes back up. I pull off my sandals and toss them onto the towering pile of junk on the passenger seat, press my bare foot against the gas—faster. *Get there. Get there. Get there.*

I look for a playground where we can stop for lunch, but the free Park Finder app that I downloaded onto the borrowed phone keeps leading me astray, promising parks where there are none to be found. When we do finally find one off an exit in the wide lower half of Georgia, it's under construction, the play structure netted off with caution tape and plastic orange fencing. By then Liam has given up entirely and fallen asleep, his hair looking almost white in the waves of sunshine coming through the van window. Dane makes a valiant attempt at a tantrum, but he's too tired to do it justice. "I know," I say. "It stinks." I slow next to a pickup at a stoplight as I drive back toward the highway. There is a handsome man in the front seat who grins and nods at me. I look at him for a fraction of a second too long—and then turn away.

"We'll find another park soon, I'm sure of it," I tell Dane. I look back at my son to see if the promise of "soon" is enough, but he, too, has fallen fast asleep, mouth slightly open, the pecans he collected this morning in my cousin's backyard still clutched in his hands.

I sigh and look resolutely out the driver's-side window so that I won't be tempted to look and see if the guy is still checking me out. Beyond the window, small neighborhoods are bordered with green landscaping and blossoming flowers. In this small highway town in Georgia, the trees are wreathed in pastel pink flowers. The magnolias are blooming. In February. I look at them for the longest time—their tissue-thin petals that shade of pink you can't replicate outside of nature—and I wonder what it would be like to live somewhere like this. Somewhere where *winter* is a short blip, a quick dip into the low fifties before the magnolias come back out and the world shimmers anew. Would I feel different in a place like this? Would I feel less heavy, less shadowed, less sad?

Someone lets out a friendly honk, and I worry for a second that it's the guy in the truck. But when I look back through the windshield, I see that he's gone, that the light has turned green—that the honking was just the car behind me trying to jolt me out of my daydream.

I wave an apology into the rearview mirror and drive on.

Back on the highway, the sun glints through the window and bathes the flattened highway land in light. Billboards advertise the world's best pecan pie and Georgia peaches, freshly picked, and outlet malls. Antiques. Pilot Travel Centers with CLEAN REST-ROOMS!

In the middle-south of Georgia, the billboards are selling a lot of things—the foremost of which is Jesus. An organization called 855-FOR-TRUTH has gone a little crazy with the ads here in the Peach State. LUST DRAGS YOU DOWN TO HELL, one of them says, with the word *HELL* burning in a wreath of menacing orange flames. Another has the evolutionary process of monkey to man in a circle, crossed out in red. IN THE BEGINNING GOD CREATED, it says next to a glowing picture of the earth.

I note the billboards for a while longer, and then I stop caring about them altogether and flip the power button on the stereo and return to *Loving Frank*. Mamah is in Europe now, traveling with her lover—Frank Lloyd Wright. She's at a lecture, listening to Ellen Key, a preeminent voice in the women's movement in Europe, and she is rapt. Key's cool voice is giving logic to the decisions that Mamah has made—leaving her husband, her children—disappearing to France with the also-married architect whom she loves.

But according to the matronly, gray-haired woman at the lectern, a marriage is dead once love has left it. It's no longer sacred, she says to the room full of women, and you must fight for your right to a love that "joins the spiritual with the erotic."

"Mamah, this is ridiculous," I tell the spinning CD. "You are smarter than this. Turn your bullshit detector back on already." But Mamah is lapping up Key's words like water—straining to hear every one of them, feeling vindicated and warm and understood.

She's still getting letters from her husband, her children. *"Come home. I still love you,"* the letters say, but for Mamah the truth is not her marriage, not the family she left behind. It's the thrumming of her own heart, the thrill of the affair, the woman at the lectern telling her that her marriage is dead if she doesn't feel it anymore.

I think about the time when it felt as if love had left my own marriage. It hadn't, of course. It had just settled a bit, changed, gotten a little tougher, a little deeper. It had felt as though my marriage was dead, but in the end it was just changing.

Back on the audiobook, though, Joyce is telling me about how Mamah has become a disciple of the famed Ellen Key, deciding to devote her professional capabilities to translating all of Key's seminal works into American English. I listen for a while, but before long, Key's theories and teachings begin to grate, and I grow to hate the narrator's rendering of her stark Swedish accent. I flip off the stereo and open the window, hoping the whooshing seventy-eight-mile-per-hour wind doesn't wake the kids.

I hold my hand out, and the warm Georgia air presses against it with a smooth forcefulness. The sun is warm and golden, and we are just miles away from the Florida state line. Billboards for

Disney World and SeaWorld and all manner of family fun are starting to speckle the side of the road. I peek back at the boys, who are still asleep. All of it feels a little miraculous.

I've flipped on Top 40 country music—the only radio station I could find—and it's pumping, low and twangy, through the speakers. I'm half listening to a song that rhymes *pier* with *drink a beer,* but mostly I'm still thinking about Ellen Key. I'm thinking about *love.* The daily work of it, the laundry and dishes of it, the letting go of it. I think about Andrew back in Minnesota, scrubbing dog pee out of the mattress. About how when I feel nothing but my own numbing darkness, it's this steady, boring, beautiful love that carries me through.

I roll my sore neck and remember a movie I watched once, about the disintegration of a marriage. *Take This Waltz,* it was called. In the movie the happily married main character, Margot, meets and falls for a stranger on an airplane—only to find out that he's the new neighbor across the street. What follows is the way in which Margot begins to pull away, distance herself from her marriage, giving in, slowly but resolutely, to the glimmering idea of something new. Something better. Eventually she tells her husband she's leaving, and he sits shocked and broken at their kitchen table, sun streaming in behind him. "I thought you were gonna be there when I died."

She leaves anyway. You see her walk into an empty studio apartment where her lover is waiting—the two of them being drawn together like magnets. The montage that follows of romance and sex is graphic and titillating and exciting—until it isn't. Until the new guy has lost his luster and they're sitting, not touching, on the new couch, watching the news. Until they're flossing and not looking at each other, until she's peeing in front of him and he's walking out of the bathroom. Until passion tempers and fades, and life goes on, and Margot has to figure out how to live in the new reality that she has created.

In one of the final, haunting scenes of the movie, Margot returns to her old house because Geraldine, the alcoholic sister of Margot's former husband, Lou, has had a relapse.

Margot has only just arrived when Geraldine comes screeching up to her house, parking her car half on the sidewalk and hitting a bunch of garbage cans. Geraldine stumbles out of the car—clearly plastered—and her face falls when she sees the policemen waiting for her next to her husband. "Oh, God. Just a sec," she says, reaching into the back of the car to pull out a box of baby chicks that she's drunkenly purchased for her daughter from the pet store. "Look, James," she says to her husband. "I got chicks. They need . . . uh . . . milk . . . I think." And it would almost be funny if James weren't looking at her with the most devastating kind of heartbreak etched across his face.

And then she sees Margot. "Heyyyyyy. How you doin'? I haven't seen you in a real long time. *A really long time,*" she says, stumbling up the porch and flinging a skinny arm around her former sister-in-law. "Is this what it takes to get you back? How you been?"

"What happened, Geraldine?" Margot asks in a low, solemn voice. In the movie you can see only her profile—that serious face, the short, wavy hair, the yellow checked shirt.

"I'm an alcoholic, moron. Nothing happened. This is my natural state," Geraldine says, her eyes rheumy with tequila, her body swaying in the sun. Then her voice gets a little more serious. "What . . . what happened? *Really?* Why wouldn't I ask that of you? You just disappeared, Margot. . . . You think everything can be worked out if you just make the right move? That must be thrilling. I think it's thrilling."

Margot looks at Geraldine with a mix of pity and disgust, and Geraldine fixes her with a piercingly clear gaze. Then she says this line that I've never forgotten, that rolls through my head now as I near the Georgia state line: "Life has a gap in it. It just does. You don't go crazy trying to fill it like some lunatic."

Geraldine walks away then, allows herself to be pushed into

the back of the police car and carted off, and Margot stands there, struck, watching her go. I'm thinking about that moment when I look up and see another 855-FOR-TRUTH billboard like a giant scab on the landscape, its bad image of Jesus's thorn-crowned head rising bloody and swollen from the cross over the words JESUS . . . YOUR ONLY WAY TO GOD.

If the image is supposed to shock me into awareness, it fails. After all, I grew up with that picture of Jesus, bloody and swollen and killed dead for my sins. Again and again in Sunday school and at summer camp and retreats and conferences, I heard the Gospel message explained like this: Jesus's death and resurrection bridge the gap between humans and God. I learned to draw it like a diagram: two cliffs—us on one side, God on the other. No way to get over to the other side except that empty cross—which is actually a bridge.

And while for some this might be a helpful image, for me it only ever confused things. I'd "prayed the prayer." I'd "asked Jesus into my heart." If the diagram were to be believed, I'd been safely across the canyon with God for fifteen years now. I'd plugged up the "God-shaped hole" that I was told exists in us all with my confession of belief, with my committed faith, with my love for Jesus. . . .

Except for the fact that I hadn't.

"Life has a gap in it. It just does," Geraldine had said—and this is what I feel so acutely now. *The gap.* In my life it has looked like a thousand different things. Loneliness. Pain. Cynicism. Depression.

Winter.

Darkness.

I feel like I've spent the last several years twisting and turning the puzzle pieces of my faith, trying to get them to plug up that "God-shaped hole" that is still throbbing like an abscess in my heart. But it never seems to go away—no matter how long I sit there, Bible in my lap, staring out the patio door of my kitchen, waiting.

I grew up evangelical, after all, and the evangelicals taught me to sing, "Jesus loves me this I know, for the Bible tells me so!" They taught me grace and love and hope and a thousand other wonderful things. But I also heard them say again and again, from the pulpit and in the church hallways and from the front of giant stadiums full of WWJD-bracelet-wearing teens, "If you feel far away from God . . . guess who moved?"

And it's this message that sits with me now as I drive down the asphalt interstate that cuts straight through the South, flanked by Jesus billboards. *Me,* I think. *I moved. I must have moved.* No matter how many times I try to talk myself out of this idea, I can't shake the thought that I must be doing it all wrong. If the God-shaped hole inside of me isn't plugged up, it must be reflective of a spiritual poverty on my part.

If it's true I've moved, then I want to move back to wherever it is that God is. But the road to my on-fire past is blocked off by time, by life, by so many things. I'm not that girl anymore—the one without a cynical or ironic bone in her body, the one who stood in a crowd of teenagers *acquiring the fire,* singing loud, calling down heaven, asking God to *just be here now.*

And so—the flirting, the men, the alcohol. "All sins are attempts to fill voids," Simone Weil said, and at some crucial point that I can't actually remember, I figured out that burning down your own life felt strikingly similar to being *on fire.* That if I couldn't shoot the gap via that bridge which is the empty cross, at least I could pour wine down into it. *Such an easy shortcut.* Such a simple fix to get tipsy on cheap cabernet and smile at some guy on some street and feel myself float to the top of that gaping, empty space in me—at least for a little while.

More signs for Disney World now and for the Florida Welcome Center, which is apparently coming up in just a few miles. A couple of billboards holler about Legoland and SeaWorld and out-let malls. I watch the signs appear and disappear and think about Margot and Geraldine, about Mamah and Ellen Key and myself. I think that maybe this whole world is full of people trying to feel something, trying to locate themselves on the flat, anonymous map of the earth. But there are times when you feel nothing, including yourself. When you are falling through a sinkhole that has opened without warning in the linoleum floor of your world.

And what are you supposed to do then? Make a move? Click through a hundred stultifying pages of porn on the Internet or stop by that strip club—the one on the billboard with the curvy silhouette? Turn off the highway at the next exit and buy a new bag or six at Tanger Outlets?

Drink the entire bottle of wine? Leave your husband for some smoldering-eyed stranger?

Pray harder? Read the Bible more? Memorize Scripture? Crank up the Christian rock on the local Fish FM station? Join another church group, make more Tater Tot hot dish for expectant moth-ers, buy another devotional book?

Throw the kids into the van and drive, drive, drive as fast as you can toward the coast?

Behind me the boys sigh in their sleep, and I turn on the radio and let the wind glide over my hand as I gun it to the state line. *FLORIDA!* When I cross it, I snap a selfie, my eyes wide, panto-miming a shout of enthusiasm that looks in the photo a little like fear.

The boys shift and lean and stay fast asleep through all of it.

Part III

Grace fills empty spaces, but it can only
enter where there is a void to receive it,
and it is grace itself which makes this void.

—Simone Weil,
GRAVITY AND GRACE

ORMOND BEACH, FLORIDA—DAY 1

Friday, February 21, 2014

The summer I turned eighteen, I used to drive to Glencoe Beach before dawn.

At that time of day, the stretch of road that connected our town to the ivy-covered mansions along the lake was empty and dark, and the stoplights were green all the way from my house to the sparkling sand of Lake Michigan. The stone steps down to the beach were shadowed by the inclined branches of the swaying ash trees, and the only sound anywhere was the soft brush of waves against land.

Looking back, I can't quite believe that my parents let me do this—sit alone on the empty beach in the early-morning dark. Every now and then, a jogger would make his way down the steps, calves taut and sweaty as he ran to the end of the dock and paused a second, hands on knees, to suck in the wet lake air before turning back toward home. But mostly it was just me on the empty white lifeguard stand in my sweatpants and sweatshirt, a modest one-piece bathing suit underneath.

From the white wooden stand that later in the day would be populated with handsome college-age lifeguards, I could watch the sky begin to light up before the sun ever appeared. The gray-purple glow streaked and bled into the black of the sky like spilled paint. The seagulls glided in, one at a time, from the ends of the horizon and landed along the shore. They stood there, perfectly still on twiggy legs, a winged congregation gathered for dawn prayer. I never could figure out why they did it—what made them come—but I assumed it was the same something that called me there, that made me set the alarm for four o'clock on the mornings of my last summer at home, that made me drive alone in the dark.

When the first light finally breached the horizon, the top of the water glowed like fire. After that it seemed to happen all at once—reds and oranges, blues and purples, a thousand shades and hues, everything sparkling. At the brightest, most electric part of the sunrise—this is where I climbed down off the lifeguard stand, stripped off my sweats, and walked shivering into the lake. This is where I raised my arms over my head and dove under, where I expected God to meet me, where I went to meet him.

How do you know God is real?

The sun shed its coat of colors, and I lay on top of the water, my skin tingling with the ecstasy of it—and the truth is that I *did* find God in those glowing mornings. I breathed in, breathed out. Floated in the silent heart of that Great Lake.

Eventually I swam to shore, deserted by then by the choir

of seagulls—a few stray feathers blowing across the sand where they'd stood. Then I sat back in the lifeguard chair, towel-wrapped and wet-haired and tingling. I wrote prayers in my journal, read psalms out of my Teen Application Study Bible, dripped lake water and love all over the place.

Because you've felt him.

What I wanted was to be as close as possible to God and his radiant Light, and already I'd begun to confuse the two—the sun and God. God and the sun. My favorite Christian rock bands were telling me to shine, and Christian youth groups and music festivals all over the place were calling themselves Sonshine and Sonlight. I spent that summer trying to somehow absorb the rays of the incandescent God into every shadowed place in my heart.

I felt the sun warm on my neck like the touch of the holy. I left off the sunscreen, rolled up my jeans, lay on a blanket, glimmering with baby oil, looking up.

And what I'm trying to say is this: if you spend an entire summer—*an entire lifetime*—driving to the beach to gaze at the sun, it's bound to damage your cornea, crack into the cells of your eye structure, change the way you see things.

Spend too long staring directly into the sun and you're bound to become a little bit blind.

Friday morning I wake up in Josh and Julie's guest room, blinking in the sunshine streaming through the window. It takes a moment for me to remember where I am. The boys have crawled up into the double bed from their single air mattresses on the floor and are sprawling across my torso. Dane is squeezing my cheeks between his hands. "Come on, Mom! Come on!" they're chanting, and then I remember.

We made it. We're in Florida.

I look around me at the spare room, the sun leaving a pattern of lines on the wall as it slides through the blinds. "Can I wear shorts, Mom?" Dane asks, digging through the Florida tote, sending folded shorts and T-shirts and sweatshirts and diapers falling in rumpled piles onto the floor.

"Mmmm-hmmm," I mumble, hoisting myself up to sitting, rubbing at my eyes. My neck is stiff from all of the days of driving, my lower back flimsy and kinked like a bent pipe cleaner. I struggle over to the guest bathroom and look in the mirror. My eyes are ringed with shadows of exhaustion so dark it almost looks like I cried with mascara and didn't get it entirely off. My face is splotchy, and there seems to be a brand-new crop of grays sprouting up along a streak at the front of my head. "Yikes," I mutter under my breath.

I brush my teeth quickly and put my hair up and then hurry after Dane and Liam, who are already thumping down the stairs. "Tell me Josh is already at work," I say as I peek around the corner into the kitchen in my sweatpants and ratty T-shirt and unretouched face.

Julie laughs lightly from the kitchen counter, where she's busy making breakfast. "Already gone," she says. "But truly, he wouldn't even notice the pj's. We're pretty casual around here."

Julie is already dressed in a bathing suit, cover-up, and flip-flops. Her bright blond hair is piled high on top of her head, sloppy and stylish all at once—unlike mine, which got matted weirdly to one side of my head in the night and still doesn't look quite right. Her two older kids, Ethan and Sophie, are sitting on the couch in their pajamas, watching cartoons, and Dane and Liam jump onto the couch next to them. "What are you watchin'?" Dane asks Ethan. The baby, Emma, is sitting in her high chair, rapping a soft-topped baby spoon on the tray.

"Nice," I say, rounding the corner to join her in the kitchen. "Please tell me you're coffee people."

"In the pot." She smiles. "Help yourself. Mugs are in the cupboard right above it."

"Oh, bless you," I say, grabbing a cup. I lean against the counter in my sweatpants and take a long drink. "All the people we've stayed with so far have been non–coffee drinkers. Which is inconvenient, seeing as my brain no longer functions without it."

"Mine either." She shakes her head as she loads the kitchen island with a buffet of breakfast food. "When did that happen?"

"I blame the kids."

"Totally."

Until last night I hadn't seen Julie in nearly a decade—not since we'd both lived and taught English in China that year. At twenty-one and twenty-two, we weren't so much *friends* then as we were *acquaintances.* Colleagues. We sat at identical desks on opposite ends of the English teachers' office, silent mirror images. Around us the young Chinese teachers fluttered about, colorful and giggling, whispering indecipherable secrets in one another's ears.

While Julie sat straight at her desk and worked on lesson plans, I slouched over mine, staring out the windows. She worked closely with the teachers on the complicated, tonal pronunciation of Chinese words. I pillaged the piecemeal collection of books abandoned by former English-speaking teachers for anything that might distract me from the grayness pressing in on me through the windows of that foreign factory town. I reread all the Anne of Green Gables books and made it about twenty-five pages in *Ragtime* before ultimately switching to a giant anthology of quotations, which I read straight through like a novel.

We were so young. Neither one of us had learned to recognize desperation in ourselves—let alone in other people. She dealt with hers by pushing herself out into the city, into sweet but stunted friendships with young Chinese teachers, into her teaching—memorizing words exhaustively so that she could communicate with her students. I dealt with mine mostly by plugging my headphones into my ears and listening to Joni Mitchell's "River" over and over while staring down at the canal stretching dully toward the horizon.

In the office Julie and I exchanged pleasantries. When her

boyfriend came to town, I helped out with her classes, and when Kim came to visit me, Julie helped out with mine. At Thanksgiving she cooked the vegetables for our feast, and we sat together and were grateful.

But I never knew that she'd gone with a Chinese teacher to purchase her wedding gown—alone in translations. No photos. No girlfriends or relatives to *ooh* and *aah* and express unwanted options. Only kind nods, the polite exchange of cash and goods. A transaction.

And she never knew that I cried myself to sleep most nights on the hard mattress of the twin beds Andrew and I had pushed together in our sixth-floor flat. She didn't know that I spent hours zoned into episodes of *Friends,* which I bought pirated from hole-in-the-wall vendors—or if she did, she didn't know that I wasn't really watching them for the entertainment value. She didn't know that the sound of the Chinese news channel made me feel lost and alone and that the sound of silence made me feel like I was disappearing—so I watched all ten seasons, one candy-coated episode at a time until the six iconic characters left the apartment arm in arm, closing that lavender door with its framed peephole for the last time. And then I took out the first season and started all over again.

The version of Julie puttering around in the kitchen this morning still bears certain similarities to the girl I sort of knew in China all those years ago. Her hair is the same, and her face is still beautiful. But she's less straitlaced and angular. Her eyes have softened, and she's abandoned the long skirts of her fundamentalist upbringing for jeans and sundresses and beachy cover-ups. She's traded in those piles of student essays for Nikon camera lenses and a thriving freelance bridal-photography business.

Whatever we were pretending to be during that year in China has long since fallen away. Our bodies have stretched and widened with the births of our babies, and so has our capacity for compassion—both for ourselves and for others. We have learned that we have entire rooms inside us that we didn't know existed before, and now, in the early-morning kitchen light, we are getting a second chance to take each other in.

"I'm thinking we need to get going to the beach as soon as possible," Julie says, sliding pancakes onto a serving plate with a spatula. "I looked at the weather, and there's rain coming this afternoon. This is our window."

"Sounds like a plan."

Ormond Beach, the town where Josh and Julie live, is located on the Atlantic Ocean, just north of Daytona. It has been a refuge for winter-worn northerners ever since the Civil War—a winter playground, popular with the captains of the railroad and oil industries. John D. Rockefeller himself spent four seasons at the Ormond Hotel, where he acquired a taste for the salty air, the sun-dappled seaside. Eventually he bought his own estate there, which he called the Casements. In the latter years of his life, this is where he chose to spend his winters.

A half dozen oil tycoons can't be wrong, I think as I follow Julie's minivan out of their quiet subdivision and about ten miles to the beach. I watch out the window as suburban Ormond Beach turns into coastline. The grocery stores and gas stations are gradually replaced with giant condos and hotels and several pink-painted houses—a few with manatee-shaped mailboxes.

At the small beachside parking lot, we unload kids and lawn chairs. Buckets and strollers and towels and sand toys and sunscreen and bug spray and changes of clothes and snacks. Loaded down with the miscellany of a Beach Day, Julie and I heave ourselves down the rickety wooden boardwalk and onto the sand. The boys are already way ahead, halfway across the expanse of sand—arrows shooting madly toward the ocean.

I stand there on the sand, slung with chairs and towels and bags, and I see it. *The ocean.* I am still for a moment and watch it stretch out before us, dark and endless, the waves rolling against the shore. *We made it,* I think. *We're here.*

Dane and Liam are in the waves before I can even change them into their swimsuits or decide if it's actually warm enough to swim at all. Julie and I haul our armloads of beach gear toward the shore and drop it gracelessly in a pile. We set up our chairs and spread out towels, but a sharp wind keeps whipping through, picking up the terry-cloth towels and sending them dancing toward the water.

It's midmorning, and the sun rose a long time ago. Whatever colors it painted in the sky in its rising have long since been swallowed back into the ocean—but it's still beautiful. The water is a hundred thousand shades of blue-fading ombré toward the horizon, where the water turns such an opaque shade that it's impossible to tell where the ocean ends and the sky begins. White-haired retirees walk hand in hand up the beach, stopping every now and then to pick up a smoothed rock or shell. A man stands by the shore, casting the long line of a fishing pole over the cresting waves. Everything is muted and hazy, a watercolor of happiness. I tip my head back, and on the other side of my closed eyes the sun glows orange and bright.

Down at the water, Dane and Ethan are leaping forward and backward, chasing and being chased by the waves. At four and five, they have struck up a friendship that is easy and instant, untroubled by fear or façades or posing or hiding. There are only the waves, the sun, the simple pleasure of having someone to run next to at the water's glinting boundary. Sophie has started a sand castle. Liam is up to his waist, his jean shorts soaked through, his bare belly hanging over the snap. He's holding a bucket and a shovel, laughing with his whole body, his dimples flashing in the sun.

I sit down on my chair and watch everything unfold exactly how I'd imagined it. *I did it.* I got us here, to the ocean shore, and my boys' unrestricted joy feels like a kind of payoff, a kind of vindication, a happy ending.

The baby crawls in the sand until she's covered with it. She picks it up by the handful and shoves it into her mouth, working out the texture and the flavor, tasting the world. A couple of times we catch her racing on all fours toward the shoreline, fearless and fascinated, and we have to scoop her up and haul her back before she drowns herself in the discovery.

"So this is what you guys do in February, huh?"

"Yep," Julie says, tipping her head back on her beach chair.

"Well then," I say. "We usually like to spend February hacking snow off our car with ice picks."

"Nice." She laughs. "You guys should really think about moving here."

"Maybe so," I say. "Maybe so."

I sit by Julie in a beach chair, feeling the sun beat down on my shoulders. Everything feels resurrected—including our relationship—as we sit there side by side on the beach. Julie adjusts the heavy zoom lens of her camera to take photo after photo. The shutter snaps—*open, close, open, close*—capturing a moment that is exactly perfect. The sun bursts through the clouds, and the beach is incandescent—all of us incandescent upon it. It's a "wish you were here" postcard, a dolphin breaching, a perfectly round sand dollar.

The kids are laughing and leaping, and I am *warm*. The sun is beating down like *glory, glory, glory* . . .

And then the moment passes.

Julie and Josh's neighbor sells things out of his garage. At least that's what they think is going on. Cars come circling into their cul-de-sac at odd intervals all day long, pulling into the driveway a few houses down, leaving several minutes later. A new one is there now, two men talking in low tones that don't quite carry across the street but that sound suspect.

"I mean, I understand selling a few things on Craigslist here and there," Julie says, putting on a long-sleeved shirt over her tank top. "But this is something else entirely. This is, like, a thriving business."

"What do you think they sell?"

"I have no idea. Everything? Their garage is *full* of stuff."

"Well, that's . . . peaceful."

"*Super* peaceful." She sighs as an engine revs and an old beat-up Ford truck sputters backward out of the driveway across the cul-de-sac, its bed filled to the brim with bulky, unidentifiable junk secured under a vinyl tarp.

Julie and I are sitting on the same beach chairs that we had at the beach this morning—only now we've relocated to the dark, open mouth of the Millers' garage—minivan on one side, lawn mower on the other. We'd been at the beach for only an hour or so before the sky began to cloud over, the kids started to shiver and complain, and we were forced to turn around and head for home.

Outside, the rain is coming down gentle and steady, and the kids are running around in it in a wide, trailing circle—their hair damp, their eyelashes glistening. I pull my sweater a little tighter across my chest and sigh.

I'm still in a partial state of disbelief over the weather. Of course, I knew that it *could* rain—that such things were possible, even in Florida. That there were no guarantees. And yet I thought I had struck some cosmic deal. *I will drive thousands of miles south to find you—and you will make it GORGEOUS,* I'd told God as I packed my totes and yanked Dane out of school and gotten my tooth sanded back smooth.

For the record, this is not *gorgeous*.

This is nasty weather and Craigslist neighbors and the subtle scent of gasoline and oil wafting through the garage as we sit here in our beach chairs, shivering. This is ashen skies and goose bumps on recently shaved legs and a sunset that is hidden behind the dense fog of rain clouds. This is Minnesota without the snow. This is *winter*.

Before we came outside to let the kids run off some energy, we spent at least an hour sitting at the kitchen table, playing Play-Doh with our children—an activity I offer regularly at home but never take part in. Ever.

When we "play Play-Doh" at our place, it means me opening the lids of several colors of clay and letting Dane and Liam get everything mishmashed together into ugly grays and browns while I read a novel in the other room. It does *not* involve me helping to scoop ice cream for a pretend shop or rolling little pretend cherries out of red dough with my fingertips. At home I never sit there and say, "Can I take your order, sir?" in my silliest voice, but I did it this afternoon. After all, Julie was helping her daughter to create a Play-Doh banana split—complete with fake chocolate syrup—using a series of molds. It didn't seem right to beg off to go upstairs and catch up on my *Vampire Diaries*.

I look at the boys, streaming through the yard, screaming happily, their toes coated in grass. "Look at me, Mom!" Dane says as he does a somersault on the lawn. I watch wearily and give him a thumbs-up and a tepid smile when he's done. "No!" he screams. "I did it *wrong*! Watch again, Mommy! I gotta do it again!" He proceeds to do several somersaults, none of which are exactly right.

Alone time. I crave alone time. I dream of anonymous coffee shops where I can sit at a little round table and shove earbuds into my ears and drink a latte and be utterly singular. I want just one moment underneath the ocean waves where all the sound goes away. Just one night in a room all by myself.

Yet here I sit in the driveway, tallying time in my head. From Sunday, when we left my parents' house, to today—Friday—it has been six days and 144 hours. 8,640 minutes—each and every one of which I have spent with my children. My children whom I love with an endless, aching kind of devotion. My children whom I might strangle if they say, "Mom! Watch me!" one more time.

When I got into that van over a week ago, I expected more than one brief hour of golden sunlight when we got to Florida, more than one moment of perfect peace. I had put it all on the line. I'd taken my winter-worn, less-than-brave self and I'd shoved it into close quarters with two preschoolers. I deserved more than this. I *bargained* for more than this. The unspoken deal I'd made with God was for beauty and light and hope and healing. Not for rainy garages in the suburbs. Not for gray skies and dark nights and frayed nerves and welling frustration.

I came here because I need help, I think as the wind shifts and cold rain slants into the garage and pelts my extended legs. *Are you ever going to come? Are you ever going to show up?*

A car at the Craigslist house backfires. "I'm going to go make dinner," Julie says.

"Can I help?" I ask, uncrossing my legs and preparing to stand up.

"Nah. Relax. Enjoy your kids. And the weather." She winks, and I try to laugh, but I'm afraid it comes out as fractured as I feel.

"Okay," I say. "Will do." But she's already inside, drawing the garage door closed behind her.

Saturday, February 22, 2014

It's gray and drizzling when we pull, side by side, into the parking lot of New Smyrna Beach the next morning, but we get out of the vans anyway, Julie's family from hers, the kids and I from ours.

"It might be fine," I say, looking up at the ominous skies.

"It'll probably be fine," Julie agrees tentatively. And we shrug and help her husband, Josh, strap the littlest ones into my double stroller, shove towels and bags into the carrier beneath, and make our way to the winding wooden boardwalk that leads to the beach.

Julie suggested that we spend our Saturday at New Smyrna after Dane labored most of yesterday morning collecting seashells at Ormond Beach. "New Smyrna is a great beach for shell collecting," she'd told me, and so that morning, in spite of the iffy forecast, we rounded up our beach gear again, loaded everything back into the van, and drove an hour down the coast toward New Smyrna.

I've been to New Smyrna Beach before—a lifetime ago with my high-school youth group. It was my freshman year, and we'd taken a forty-foot, double-decker motor coach called the Lightrider from the Chicago suburbs to Florida for what felt like one giant traveling slumber party. The *t* in the word *Lightrider* was a cross, and the side of the bus was emblazoned with a gigantic American flag. The Lightrider mission statement included the phrase "Putting 'In God We Trust' Back into the American Way."

The bus rolled down the countryside, and we crowded upstairs, playing card games and giving each other back massages and singing a popular worship song called "Light the Fire" while someone strummed a guitar. Were all of our favorite songs in those days about light and fire and shining for Jesus? Or am I just imagining it now on this dismal morning as we walk toward the boardwalk?

I remember the way that the Lightrider bus always smelled a little like socks but that it didn't really bother me. During the night we praised and prayed, flirted and slept. During the day we were deposited at various tourist stops—Stone Mountain, the World of Coca-Cola, and, of course, New Smyrna Beach herself, where we swarmed out of the bus in modest one-piece swimsuits and flip-flops and ran full tilt toward the water.

Back home, snow pummeled the Chicagoland area, and my high-school friends were being forced to run a fifteen-minute loop around the field house during gym class, but I had escaped. I gripped the torso of a handsome older boy as we flew over the packed sand of New Smyrna in a rented ATV. Afterward I sat next to him, feet half buried in the sun-baked sand, as the two of us waxed poetic about Jesus. The boy's eyes were the same color as the ocean, and I felt myself going under—baptized into sunshine and first love and a faith that felt like eternal summer.

Now, sixteen years later, I'm having a hard time reconciling that memory of New Smyrna with the gray, bristled landscape around me. I push the stroller down the boardwalk, following Dane and Ethan, who are holding hands sweetly, carrying plastic buckets for shell collecting. My hair, which I curled this morning, is already hanging limp and damp against my back in the drizzle; my body feels weighed down by the stroller and all the heavy creaking responsibility as I push forward.

Before we've even made it halfway down the boardwalk to the beach, the drizzling sky yawns open, the mist that's been following us solidifying into scattered raindrops.

"Just a little rain," I say to Julie, my eyebrows crinkling as cold water droplets smack against my forehead. "It's *totally* fine."

"*Totally* fine," she agrees.

We hear it sweeping across the brush before we feel it. It sounds like the rinse cycle of a car wash beating against the windows. And then it's beating against *us*—sheets of water, drenching us in seconds.

The kids scream, and we run for a picnic shelter built into a lookout on the boardwalk. We mop at our children's shocked, wet faces with the bath towels in the stroller—"Just a little water! No big deal! There. All better!"—and then we ply them with snacks and juice boxes. Their moods have swung from expectant to sullen and sopping, and even the snacks don't do much to quell their irritation.

Dane leans toward me, holding his bag of trail mix. "What's *in* this, Mom?" he whispers.

"Nuts."

"I don't like nuts."

"And raisins."

"I hate raisins."

"And M&M's."

"I guess I like M&M's," he says sullenly, taking the bag like it's some kind of poor consolation prize and sitting down next to Ethan at the end of the picnic table. Liam, in the back of the stroller, works methodically through his bag—fishing first for chocolate, then for peanuts, then, finally, suspiciously, for raisins. He eats one piece at a time until every last crumb is gone.

"I thought you . . . checked the weather," Josh says quietly to his wife as he twists the bottom of his T-shirt to wring it out.

"I *did*," she says. "It was only a *chance* of rain."

"But what *percentage* chance?"

"Well, I don't really remember." She hands him a bag of trail mix, and he kisses her on the cheek, his damp shirt sticking to his arms. "Maybe it'll pass."

"Mmm-hmmm." He goes and sits down next to the kids, who have gone silent, watching the rain and eating their snack.

Three bags of trail mix later, the *whooshing* of water on wood slows and settles back into a drizzle. The edge of the sun is almost visible behind the wall of dark clouds, and I point to it. "Look, you guys! The sun's coming out!" I realize as I shout this that I sound like a deranged cheerleader, but I don't care. "Hooray!"

"Yay! Sun!" Julie jams the remains of the snacks into the stroller. "Let's make a run for the beach!" she shouts with mustered enthusiasm that matches mine.

The kids don't look convinced—and neither does Josh. But they allow themselves to be dragged out of the picnic shelter, down the beach stairs, and onto the sand—where the rain begins in earnest again, only this time without the shelter of the sand dunes to cut the wind. It falls cold and sharp against our bare arms. It soaks our hair and sends black lines of mascara careening down my face and Julie's while we follow our kids toward the foamy-gray shoreline.

Liam has scrambled into my arms and refuses to be let down. He burrows into my wet cardigan and mumbles, *"Go home?"* over and over again while I tentatively test the water with my toes. It feels warmer than the sky.

Dane works his way along the damp sand, collecting shells and dumping them into his pail, but I can see his thin shoulders shivering under his red sweatshirt.

"Why did you bring us here, Mom!" Ethan shouts as the waves pick up and begin to slap sharp against the shore.

"Well, we didn't think it would rain. . . ." Julie begins. Her small, brown-eyed son looks at her with an incredulous mix of doubt and pity, as if he can't believe that his own mother could be so dumb.

"This was not a great plan," he says matter-of-factly, crossing his arms over his wet shirt.

Julie and I look at each other and blink. Then we both start laughing, doubling over as rain pelts us unforgivingly, our kids looking on with open mouths. There is nothing to do but hold our stomachs and crack up as the inhospitable ocean roars and we stand, drenched, in the Shark Bite Capital of the United States.

"No," Julie admits when she finally catches her breath. She wipes at her cheek with the corner of her towel. "I guess it probably wasn't."

Josh is already gone. He'd scooped up baby Emma and made a run for the van when it became clear that her lips were actually turning a subtle shade of blue. Julie and I start making our way back toward the boardwalk, carefully avoiding beached jellyfish while haphazardly scooping up shells for Dane. Handful by small handful, we toss them into his bucket, still packed with wet white sand. This is no time for being choosy.

By the time we make it back up to the steps where we parked the stroller, we're sand-coated, soaked through, and more than a little miserable. Dane and Ethan huddle together, wrapped in pink bath towels, while Julie and I make futile attempts at brushing the sand off their feet before we finally just give up and strap Velcro sandals over the top. Sophie sits in the front of the stroller, her long ponytail drooping wet down the side of her face; Liam is in the back, buried under a damp aqua towel, looking bewildered.

It's a different kind of cold from the Minnesota winter cold that crushes through your layers and hurts in your bones. But it's still *cold*. The little ones in the stroller are silent and sullen, and Dane is hauling his bucket of sand-filled shells until he finally can't. He stops in the rainy center of the road. "Carry me, Mom," he whines.

"Oh, buddy. You're so heavy."

"Please!" he whimpers, and he looks so small and miserable, wrapped in his towel, lugging his bucket, shaking at the knees.

"I'll push the stroller," Julie offers.

"Just for a little while," I tell Dane. And then I hoist him up. He's four and a half years old, and he really is *heavy*—all arms and knees and angles. The wheels of the stroller catch on the slats of the boardwalk, marking time as Julie pushes ahead and then disappears around a turn. I slow under the weight of my older boy, his solid body pinning me to the rain-drenched world. He plants his sharp chin on top of my shoulder, and I can feel his chattering breath against my ear. I clutch him tighter, hoisting him higher on my hip bone to disperse the weight as the rain *tap-tap-taps* against the boardwalk.

I would have been fourteen that winter, when the Lightrider bus pulled into New Smyrna Beach. I'd been in high school for only half a year, but I'd already learned to echo the repeating refrain of our favorite worship song:

> *Light the fire in my soul*
> *Fan the flame make me whole*

It wasn't just a song. It was a *mantra* for everything we were taught to want, which most of all was to be *on-fire-in-love with God*. Spiky-haired, sneaker-wearing youth-group leaders spent a lot of time encouraging us to be *all in*, to be *sold out*, to live with a passionate faith, shining and sparkling for all the world to see. And I was great at it.

Being *on fire* was not a subtle affair. It was consuming and big and bright. It looked like regular "quiet times" in the early morning, like teary-eyed insights offered during Bible study, like T-shirts with Jesus-y messages and WWJD bracelets and belting Sonicflood's "I Could Sing of Your Love Forever" at the top of your lungs in the car. The Church People looked on with approving eyes, made me the poster child, put me on a pedestal that I learned to love. *This is what faith should look like,* they told the kids who were half committed, who spent their weekends drinking and listening to Green Day.

I'm not saying my feelings weren't real. *They were.* But that kind of sudden, unmitigated approval can be dangerous—as addictive and toxic as any drug. I was really just a teenager, learning to take her first fumbling steps toward faith. But from the top of that spiritual pedestal, I began to believe that I'd already arrived. I led small groups and Bible studies and peer prayer groups and mission-trip dramas. I was added to leadership teams and asked to mentor younger women. I thought I understood it all.

In reality those years required little of me in the way of actual faith. I drove to the beach in the earliest mornings to meet God, to find him—and I always did. When I opened the Bible, I heard God speak in a near-audible whisper. The worship music crescendoed around me, and I couldn't have felt nearer to God if angels had been standing right there beating their giant wings and glowing white.

That song—the one we all loved—also talks about weariness, about having your faith leached out of you. But the idea of a deep faith-weariness felt foreign to me. It felt incomprehensibly terrible then, and when I echoed the lyrics of the worship song at fifteen and sixteen and seventeen, I sang them with desperation.

I wish someone had told me then that eventually the fire would go out *and that it would be okay.* That it didn't mean my faith was dying. I wish someone had told me that the fire doesn't make me whole, that I am whole because of Jesus, whether I feel him or not.

Tap-tap-tap goes the rain. Julie is gone, and there is not another person in sight. There is only the gray and green of the sand dunes and the constant winter rain running down our faces. My face is tilted up to the sky, but there's no sun, no fire, no flame fanning through the Florida brush to make me whole. Just this gray rain, tapping all around us.

"I can only carry you for a few more minutes," I tell Dane, but he clings tighter to my torso. The dense drizzle cuts through my cardigan, making it stick as if glued to my arms. "Seriously, dude. You're so heavy. You're getting to be *so big.*"

He sighs in my ear. "I know. It's because I'm four."

"Yes. You are," I say, and kiss his rain-soaked head. "When did that happen?"

In spite of myself, I carry him all the way back to the parking lot. Above us the sky is heavy with veiled glory, and the winter rains might sound like the whispering breath of God if only I knew how to listen. As it is, I'm too cold and crabby and disappointed to hear the song of the sodden beach, the lullaby that God sings over all that he has made, the God of light and dark, sun and rain, whispering across the sand dunes: *I am here, I am here, I am here.*

At the center of Josh and Julie's quiet subdivision, there is a man-made pond with a fountain. The pond is eerily still. Even the fountain barely seems to rumple the surface of the water, and there's not a single duck or goose gliding across. Cars drive by every once in a while, but even their engines seem quieted, as if someone has pushed a mute button on the whole neighborhood this warm, gray Saturday afternoon.

This is where Dane, Liam, and I end up a few hours after the New Smyrna Incident, when the entire Miller family settles down for a nap. I'd hoped my kids would rest, too, but they were re-energized after a hot bath and a warm lunch. Instead of watching a movie on my computer as I hoped they would, they scuttled around the bed like sand crabs, pinching each other and then shrieking with laughter.

"Out!" I'd whispered, wresting my tired body from the bed. "You're going to wake up baby Emma! Get your shoes on. We're going for a walk!"

In the Millers' subdivision, the sky is gunmetal gray, but it's no longer raining. A mail truck trundles by, but the postal worker doesn't wave. I turn the stroller toward the pond, where a short boardwalk leads out to a gazebo. From here I can see the backs of the suburban houses, each boasting an attached screened-in porch—all of them empty. The whole place feels apocalyptic in its stillness, *end-of-the-world* lonely.

Dane and Liam don't notice. They pick their way down right next to the pond, where they crouch on hands and knees, looking for treasures. One by one they bring me sticks and rocks. Leaves. Bits of clover. "Keep this safe, Mom," Dane tells me. "Save it for me."

"Okay," I tell him, and I put the collected fragments of Florida pond life in a pile on my lap. I twist the thin, gnarled torso of a twig between my fingers as I watch my children play. I try to call Andrew, but the phone rings four times and then clicks over to his voice-mail message. "Hi . . . You've reached Andrew Zierman. . . ."

"Hey, sweets," I say when it beeps. "I'm guessing that you're probably taking a Saturday-afternoon nap. Which is great. I'm just really happy for you about that." I let my voice drip with as much good-natured sarcasm as I can muster. "Let me tell you about *our* morning. We drove an hour to check out a new beach—and got caught in a *monsoon*. And the kids won't nap. *Julie's* kids nap. Why don't *our* kids nap?

I take a breath, and the suburban silence buzzes into the phone.

"Anyway . . ." I say to the recording. "I'm sitting here in the middle of Julie and Josh's neighborhood at this little pond, and the kids are collecting stuff. Not exactly the ocean, but it seems to be doing the trick for now. We'll bring you home some . . . moss."

The kids are giggling as they touch the tips of their shoes to the mucky pond water and then looking at me to see if I'm going to do anything about it. I probably should, but I don't have the energy. "Okay. Wish you were here. Call me later."

I click the End button on the call and then cast idly around the Square apps of my iPhone for something to do. When I log into Facebook, it tells me, *Today is your friend Stephen's birthday!* and suggests that I write on his wall. I lean my head against the wooden railing and look at the sky, but my old friend's name is a blue road sign pointing me down the back roads of my past. *Stephen.*

It was just *Steve* then, when I knew him best. He was the boy who was sitting beside the foosball table at that youth church, Vertical Connection, the first time I came in. "'Sup," he'd said. "Not much," I'd replied, tucking my hair nervously behind my ear, and then, inexplicably, we were friends, and we spent the next four years being on fire for God—together.

I close my eyes and I can see the fifteen-year-old version of Steve—Stephen—so clearly. Spiked black hair, frosted at the tips. That metal-ball choker. That affectionate way he hugged me around the neck and called me "kid." He was next to me during youth church, jumping up and down to the ska versions of worship songs. He was across from me at a table at Denny's, and we were talking about starting a Christian zine at our high schools, our voices escalating as we imagined how it would be when everyone read it and finally *got Jesus.*

After graduation Steve and I lost touch, and it was only a few years ago through Facebook that we'd found each other again. He had become *Stephen* by then, and he lived in Denmark with his wife, Dawn. I watched his life scroll by over the next months and years in photos on my Facebook feed, his wife's pregnant belly growing, growing, growing, and then—baby Hope blinking onto the screen with her dad's eyes and her mama's lips. Hope in the bathtub, Hope on the swing. Several months more and then photos of a brand-new baby—a beautiful little boy named Esben—tucked under Stephen's chin, both father and son fast asleep.

Here is what you don't imagine will happen to you when you are seventeen and raising your arms and singing praise songs in the haze of the fog machine: You don't imagine aneurysms. You don't imagine a bleed in the brain stem and a damaged spinal cord. You've never even heard of the phrase *incomplete quadriplegic.* But this is what happened to Steve just a few months ago.

At seventeen the only chronic pain I knew about was that of my various breakups. But now I understand that it's something different. Something searing and constant and intense. Something that keeps you awake at night, coursing through your body like molten lava.

I look at my phone again. *Today is your friend Stephen's birthday!* Of course it is: 2.22. He'd always liked the poetry of that, the symmetry of all those twos marking the anniversary of his birth. *Happy birthday, kid,* I think as I regard the phone.

"Mom! Look!" Dane says, and he's holding up a broken root, torn from the ground.

"Oh, honey. That's cool, but roots need to stay *in the ground,* or the trees can't grow."

"Oh," he says, eyeing the spindled dirt clod in his hand. "Okay, Mom."

I tap a quick birthday message to Stephen in the Facebook window, while behind me the fountain churns the water and the kids' footsteps crunch under the trees below. What can I wish him on this day, in this impossible situation? Certainly not anything as simple as "Happy birthday." Happiness is too thin a word. I stare at the screen for a while before writing something fluffy and sentimental and insufficient. *"Wishing you a 31st year that is filled with sunbursts of grace, beauty, and hope."*

After I type it, I reread it and cringe at my use of the word *sunbursts.* The truth is that Stephen's life will now forever include a certain amount of darkness. So will his family's life. *Chronic pain* means that there's no getting through, no other side, no future scenario in which this is all behind them.

I don't mean to sound dismal, hopeless, dismissive. Of course light bursts through still. *Of course it does.* Life is still beautiful, and God is still good, and Stephen's toddler will crawl into bed with him and Dawn and leave sloppy kisses on their cheeks. Stephen will learn to navigate his new normal with a fancy wheelchair and a host of medication lined up for him every morning, little soldiers, showing up for duty. The medicine will sometimes help.

He'll meet wonderful people in rehab. He'll learn new things about God and life and grace and beauty. From his spot on the seat of his wheelchair, he'll see the world in a different way, and it will leave him breathless sometimes. He'll look at his wife across the room, and he'll hear his daughter sing made-up songs, and it will be *beautiful.* It will be almost enough.

I sigh and glance down at my kids, sitting under the heavy gray sky, intent on the sticks and dirt around them.

Is this what faith is now? In the aftermath of those on-fire days of first faith, first love, is all we can hope for *sunbursts*? Bright moments of grace and beauty appearing every few miles on a dark stretch of highway, reminding you that there's more than this? That the road is not all there is? That you're headed somewhere else, somewhere better, somewhere brighter and warmer and eternal and perfect?

It's not untrue—and there's a certain amount of beauty to the concept. And yet . . . what about the in-between? The dark stretches? The nights of agonizing pain when the medicine doesn't take the edge off? When instead the edge cuts into you like a sharpened knife?

What about the months of cold, when the temps keep falling lower into the negatives and you see your reflection in the glare ice on the road and you find yourself totally and completely numb?

How do you know God is real?

I look back at my phone and scroll idly through pictures of Stephen in his wheelchair, in his hospital bed, in rehab, trying to learn how to move again with what he calls his "bionic leg." He has a thick, black beard now, and behind his hipster glasses his eyes look tired and anguished even when he smiles.

I stop at a picture of his wife, Dawn—a profile shot of her midbite at a restaurant on Valentine's Day. Her dark bangs brush against her forehead and a laugh plays at her lips, which are closed around a fork. But I think there's something else that I can't quite put my finger on—exhaustion? Loneliness? Fear?

I wonder if she lies awake at night listening to her husband shift and breathe and moan. I wonder if she feels his pain radiating out until it covers her, too, and isolating her from everyone else. Does she feel God anymore? Or does she find herself disappearing into an endless tunnel of darkness, with no light at the end? Wash the dishes, dress the kids, pick up prescriptions, and wait for a miracle that never seems to come.

I wonder if she ever feels like putting the kids in the car and driving far, far away.

I wonder if people tell her that she's brave.

How do you know God is real?

Back home in Minnesota, it's another day of subzero temperatures and slicing windchills. A week from now, we'll be back there, and any relief I found in the southern sun will have faded along with whatever tiny tan I might have secured. It's only February, and whether or not that groundhog in Punxsutawney, Pennsylvania, saw his shadow at the beginning of the month is irrelevant.

In Minnesota, winter stretches six more weeks, eight more weeks, twelve, sixteen. It lasts as long as it lasts. Longer than it should—like grief, like pain, like any kind of loss.

How do you know God is real?

Because you've FELT him.

Over by the pond, the kids are coated with mud, surrounded by rocks. I turn off the phone and lie down on the hard wooden bench at the end of the boardwalk. The sky is an infinite empty slate, and there is no sound at all except for the unproductive patter of the fountain, cycling the same water through again and again. Even the boys are quiet in their exploration. I shiver in the afternoon chill and cross my arms over my chest. I close my eyes, and I am a root, pulled up from the ground, disconnected from everything.

I feel nothing. Nothing at all.

Later that night Josh is zoned in on the Olympic ice hockey men's semifinal between the USA and Canada. Theirs is an intense rivalry, Canada having won the gold twice, beating the USA both times. And Josh is a Canadian by birth, and no amount of Florida sunshine can sway him from his national pride as he yells at the screen, "Come on!"

On the TV red and white jerseys glide across the ice, slamming into one another. The hockey sticks clack desperately against the ice, while behind the purple banners of the Sochi ice arena the crowd screams madly. A goal is made, and Josh lets out a whoop, while back in Sochi the game has already been won or lost and the Olympic athletes are lying in unfamiliar beds, unsleeping—remembering the glory or the pain.

Julie and I are draped over the couches in our sweatpants, tired from the wild, rainy day, companionably quiet. In the last two days, we have rehashed most of our memories of China, filled each other in on the ups and downs of the past decade, compared notes on parenting, and lamented our gray hairs. It has taken just two days to cross that distance that once seemed to span a hundred thousand miles and the Chinese English teachers' office—the distance between acquaintances and friends.

Now we shovel barbecue-flavored popcorn into our mouths and bemoan today's terrible weather. We sit there half watching the game, mostly recalling our failed beach trip.

"Their faces when we got down to the beach!" I say, shaking my head.

"Oh, my gosh. Emma was *purple*," Julie says. She's curled up next to Josh, her hair in a topknot, her face lit with a broad smile. "I've never seen a human being quite that color before." Her voice edges toward hysterical laughter.

"*Mom! Why did you bring us here?!*" I say, doing my best imitation of a disgruntled five-year-old.

"*This was not a great plan!*" Julie replies, and we get the giggles all over again. I can see us—drowned rats with makeup-blackened eyes, hauling our waterlogged kids up the beach. And maybe it's exhaustion or the warm living room, or maybe it's the sheer absurdity of driving 1,702.2 miles, only to end up shivering in the rain. Whatever it is, I can't stop laughing.

We sit there talking and half watching TV until Canada has won the game and all the popcorn is gone, until our laughter gives way to yawns.

When Julie and Josh disappear into their bedroom, I wander outside, barefooted, to the van. On the way home from the beach, I stopped at Walgreens to buy a contact case—but mostly to buy myself cheap wine. Somewhere between the greeting cards and the refrigerated dairy products, I'd found four-pack bottles of Sutter Home, and I'd picked up the cabernet immediately. I brought one of the little bottles inside with me earlier, and I drank it slowly and restrainedly from a tumbler while we watched the hockey game. But now Julie and Josh are sleeping, and there are three little bottles of wine on the passenger seat.

I'm in a strange, dark mood that has its roots in either the beach trip from hell or the afternoon at the fountain pond, looking at pictures of Stephen alone in his wheelchair at the harbor. Or, more likely, in my own rootless sense of loneliness. And there are three small bottles of wine in the car. And I'm going out to get them.

Outside, the moon is half lit—53 percent visible, twenty-two days old. It casts long shadows on the manicured lawns of the neighborhood houses and over the packed driveway of the Craigslist people, who seem to be making a sale right now.

I get my wine out of the van, and then I lean against the car door and breathe in the silence. Fractured as the moon is tonight, dull as its asphalt surface makes it, poor as its reflection of the sun might be . . . it's still so bright. It's a quarter of a million miles away, but it looks so close—just over the houses, just a few miles away, *just there*—at the horizon, pulling the ocean water like a magnet, creating tides.

The kids and I leave for home the day after tomorrow, and I've barely glimpsed the sun at all. We'd come with the rain, with the clouds. I'd come to the shoreline to meet God like I used to do at eighteen—but I'd come too late. I'd missed it, missed whatever miracle I'd hoped to find, missed whatever Hallmark-esque "sunburst" of healing I thought would be waiting here for us.

I pull a small bottle of cabernet out of its cardboard carrier, screw off the lid, and take a long drink. I do it even though I know that my relationship with wine is complicated. Even though I can tell that I'm feeling bingey and that it can lead nowhere good. Even though I *know* that when the sadness gets under my skin like this, I tend to go overboard trying to drown it in booze and then wake up the next day with a hefty amount of regret— and also a hangover. I do it anyway.

Tonight the darkness is heavy and humid around me, and the broken-open moon is pulling me forward, and the gap is too much for me. I stand there breathing it in, looking for stars in the thrown light of the coastal city, but it's too bright, and I'm too tired.

A motor starts at the Craigslist house, and I screw the cap back onto the little wine bottle and head into the house. I tiptoe up the stairs to the guest bedroom, where I can turn on my computer and stick in my earbuds. Where I can watch some dramatic TV show capitalize on the world's brokenness, spin it off into forty-minute episodes that never seem to resolve.

Where I can drink wine until I beige out altogether, numb myself to the sharpness of the day, and where I can eventually, finally, fall asleep.

Sunday, February 23, 2014

It's Sunday morning, and the Miller family is dressed up—color-coordinated, hair curled, headed to church.

The Zierman family is not. We are in bathing suits and tank tops and sandaled feet and towels. The morning forecast is *sunshine,* and it's our last day in Florida. "We'll worship God at the beach," I say mindlessly to Julie, tossing my hair into a messy, unglamorous pile on my head in the vaulted entryway where we're both getting our shoes on. I drank only one extra little bottle of wine last night—two total—before I passed out, but still I have a terrible headache that seems to extend all the way into my teeth this morning. I blame it on the quality of the wine—*oh, Sutter Home*—instead of my own, bingey lack of restraint.

"It's a gorgeous day. You *definitely* need to go to the beach." Julie pulls on a pretty beige heel and grins at me.

I look out the windows on either side of the front door as I jam dry towels into our beach bag. It's sunny now, but there are clouds on the horizon after lunch today. We've come 1,702.2 miles, and this is our last chance. *My* last chance.

Ormond Beach is almost entirely empty when we get there twenty minutes later. The sand is soft and packed down like measured brown sugar, mostly unmarred even though it's already late morning. "Yessss!" Dane says when he sees the water, pumping his fist into the air, and then the boys fling off their shoes and go running for the waves, leaving smudgy wet footprints in their wake. I follow them, sunglasses perched at the top of my head, breathing in deep the sea air.

The tide is out, the water bluer than the throbbing center of a bruise. At the perimeter of the morning light, I can just barely see the whitewashed half-moon, ghostly in the sky. It's nearly invisible, but it's there just as surely as the sun, pulling water and earth toward itself. And the ocean water, fluid and untethered as love, allows herself to be pulled.

Low tide.

Dane is in the waves immediately, filling a plastic bucket with water and flinging it into the air so that the sky above him seems to be filling with a hundred thousand tiny diamonds, falling. "Take a picture of me, Mom!" he shouts over the water, and I do. Again and again I photograph his slight frame, his wind-tousled hair, all of him shimmering in the silver morning light of sun and water. I know that I can't capture it—this moment, this joy—but I try anyway.

Liam is less sure this time about the ocean. He stops running well before he gets to the waterline, and then he scrambles up into my arms. "Cold?" he keeps asking over and over.

"It's not too cold," I tell him. "See?" I scoop a handful of foamy water from the incoming tide into my cupped hand and let it dribble gently down his dimpled foot. He looks curiously at it and then at me—his blue eyes squinting quizzically in the sun—but he still doesn't get down. He keeps looking around, as if he's waiting for the sky to break open and dump all over us the way it did yesterday.

Finally he slips down from my arms and makes his way toward the water. First just toes. Then entire chubby legs. Then, all at once, he's running in and out of the water, laughing so hard that his cheap camouflage swim trunks droop and fall past his swim diaper.

I snap a picture—my boys, silhouettes against the sun-soaked sky. Shadow dancers at low tide. Dark and light.

"That'll turn out cute!" a woman's voice hollers from somewhere behind me. I turn around and see her stretched out on a blanket on her stomach—late middle age, looking almost Cher-like in her yoga pants and tank top and long, dark, flat-ironed hair.

I peer down at the image I've just captured on the phone, turn it off, and tuck it securely back into the zippered pocket inside my beach bag. "Yeah. Hopefully!"

"How old are they?" she yells again.

"Four and two." On the beach blanket next to the woman is an open Bible, which she has been reading, but now that she's made contact, she stands up and brushes off her yoga pants as she walks toward me.

"I have a granddaughter that age," she says, coming to stand next to me. "She has *lots* to say."

I smile and nod. "I'll bet."

The woman tells me that her name is Donna, and she *also* seems to have lots to say. She talks in drawn-out, breathless sentences, as if she's been quiet for too long. Her voice is low and gravelly, like she's been chain-smoking for many years, and the wrinkles around her mouth are deep. So is her worry line, I can't help but notice.

Donna tells me that it's her birthday, but she doesn't leave space between sentences for me to wish her a happy one. She tells me that tonight her pastor and all her friends are throwing her a party at a restaurant. "Isn't that just the nicest thing?" she coos, and I nod.

"Very nice."

"I live out in Gainesville. You know it?"

"I don't. I haven't spent much time down here."

"Central Florida," she explains, dragging her toes to cut lines in the sand. "I got off work last night and thought to myself, 'I need to see the ocean.' So I drove here and spent the night in my car in the parking lot."

"Wow. Good for you." I look at Donna, bleary-eyed and happy, and I can't help thinking about my eighteen-year-old self, driving half an hour at four in the morning to watch the sunrise over Lake Michigan. My *current self*, dragging her kids down the ridged backbone of the country to be here, in this sun-soaked moment. If anyone knows something about the draw of sun and water, it's me.

Still, the way she angles herself toward me makes me shift backward. "You must be Minnesota," she says.

"How'd you know? Am I that pale?"

She laughs. "Nah. Saw your plates in the parking lot."

"Ah." I nod. "Yes. We're Minnesota. Just down for the weekend for . . ." I falter briefly. "Some sun."

"That's a long drive."

"Yep."

"You must be brave."

"Must be." I kick at the sand with my bare toes and watch as Liam decides he's had it with his droopy swim trunks, strips them off, and proceeds to run into the waves in just his swim diaper. "Happy birthday, by the way!" I say, changing the subject, not really wanting to get into my road trip or my nebulous reasons for taking it. "Nice of your pastor to arrange a party for you."

"Yeah. It's a great church," she says, and I feel her posture change. She looks me over, and I get the distinct feeling that she's trying to suss out whether or not I'm in need of the Gospel message. Apparently she decides yes, because she brushes a long strand of dark hair behind her ear, looks at me meaningfully, and says, "What about you? Do you go to church?"

I hesitate, the question feeling like a loaded weapon aimed at my head.

There are so many things I could tell her in this moment. I could tell her that I actually wrote the book on going to church . . . and leaving church . . . and going back to church. *Literally.* And then, if I wanted, I could tell her the whole long story. I could tell her about growing up *on fire for Jesus,* about the girl who felt God always like the gently glowing sun. I could tell her how it all started crumbling—imperceptibly at first, each bad church experience chipping away one small piece of my childlike faith—until the whole thing was dangerously unstable at the foundation.

I could tell her about the moment when it all finally fell apart. About the Man Who Was Not My Husband and about the crushing Bottom Place, where I felt like I was suffocating in a dark chasm of my own making.

And then I could tell her about getting better, about the counseling and the long, teary-eyed conversations. About my babies, who came crashing, one after another, into the walls I'd built around my heart, breaking me open. About the tiny community church that we go to now—the one that's like water in the wilderness—a spring bursting out of what I thought was just a rock.

"We do go to church," I say, and if I were really *brave,* the way everyone says, I might tell her about what it's like *now*—about how even though so much has been healed, there's so much that hasn't. That I still don't really know how to navigate my soul's winter seasons. That so often I feel stripped bare like a dormant elm. That I don't really know how to trust in God when I can't feel him, so I drink one more glass of cabernet or I look a moment too long into the thick-lashed eyes of the man in the car next to me—or I run away to the ocean so that I can feel . . . *something.* Anything. Even if what I feel is my own self-destruction.

"That's good," she says, and I realize that I've told her only the iceberg tip of truth. Just that we go to church. Nothing real. Nothing else.

"Yeah, it is," I say finally.

"My church is charismatic," she says, but then she looks at me and backpedals a little. "Not like *weird* charismatic. I mean, our church is really cool. We just really want to love on people, you know?"

"Mmm," I say, suppressing a laugh. The line is so comically familiar, and I have a sudden acute memory of using it myself with the same conspiratorial side eyes that she has now. *Yeah, I'm a Christian. But not, you know, a* weird *Christian,* I'd say as I wandered the streets of foreign cities, still in costume from a flash Gospel drama that my youth group had just performed in pedestrian traffic. *It's not really religion,* I'd say, sidling up to a classmate in the hall after standing for an hour by the school flagpole to pray. *It's more like a relationship.* As though that made it cooler, more normal, more relevant.

But Donna's talking now, about finding Jesus—a new story, freshly imprinted upon her heart. Her dark eyes are wide with it, still full of those first golden tinges of awe and gratitude and disbelief. She tells me about her own checkered path to God—her rebellious daughter, her broken marriage, her messy life. She sighs and talks about how she worries about her granddaughter, living in the instabilities of her mother's bad decisions. I can see the regret playing at the edges of Donna's eyes before she snaps back to the script. "But I know that God has a plan," she says. "He won't give us more than we can handle."

As she says this, a renegade wave appears out of nowhere. It rushes wildly toward where we stand, a good fifty feet from where the waves had been breaking. Before we can grab her blanket, the wave is sweeping into it—dousing her bags and her books and her still-open Bible. Donna is laughing as we lunge for soaking shoes and sweatshirts.

"Well!" she says when she finally catches her breath. "Speaking of God!"

"Mom!" I hear Dane shout from the spot several yards up the beach where I left our pile of stuff. There, on the cusp of the receding wave, floats my blue-and-white-striped beach bag. The one holding our clothes, the car keys—and, of course, the iPhone borrowed from my cousin in Georgia.

Noooooooo.

I drop Donna's beach blanket and sprint toward our stuff, my bare feet sinking divots into the now-soaking sand. By the time I get to the bag, it's been carried two feet toward the shore on the turned back of that mammoth wave. The whole thing is soaked.

Donna is right behind me when I stoop to pick it up. She's still laughing, and I sort of want to throttle her. I pull out the iPhone, which is damp on the case, and hastily dry it on my T-shirt. *Don't let it be broken,* I pray desperately under my breath as Donna tries to quell her laughter. I push the button, and the screen lights up, and I release an uneasy sigh of relief. At least it's turning on.

Donna catches her breath and makes a hasty, insincere apology. "I'm sorry. Your phone okay?"

"I sure hope so."

"Well! Doesn't God show up in miraculous ways?!"

I look at Donna, and I'm sure that my face is a tableau of disbelief and, quite possibly, thinly veiled hatred. But she doesn't seem to notice. She glows with certainty and sunshine, and that homesick part of me rises up in a wave of its own: nostalgia for those early days of my adolescent faith—when the world was flat and limitless, and God was waiting for me at the beach every morning, and everything made sense. Now the world beneath my feet has curved and disappeared into the wilderness. It has become something more complex and terrifying and cold and dark.

Donna and I, we might as well be on two different sides of the world. She sees God now, bright as the sunshine. I can barely make out the broken face of the moon.

I wander idly around, gathering up soaked and scattered beach stuff. I don't really want to leave, but I want to stop hanging out with Donna, and leaving seems like the only way to shake her. Donna is oblivious to my frustration, talking about miracles and the ways that God always shows up. I nod absently, interrupting her several times to call for the boys, who are back in the water. "Come on, you two! Time to go!"

"Here!" she exclaims, her eyes suddenly lighting. "I'll make a sand castle. Kids *love* sand castles." I'm about to tell her it's unnecessary, that we don't really have time, but she's already kneeling down and scooping sand into a bucket, her damp yoga pants already caked.

"Thanks," I say, watching for a moment as she lets the sand fall through her fingers. It's her gift of kindness, her offering of love, and my sharp frustration dulls against the generosity of this moment. I look at Donna and find myself flooded with compassion—for her, for me, for every person tramping through the changing topography of faith.

Donna—she's *on fire* for Jesus, driving to the ocean in the middle of the night to meet him like a lover. She's waiting at the beach at sunrise with the seabirds, beginning her journey with God. Her heart is a match struck for the first time against the rough goodness of grace. She is still smiling in the afterglow of the wave—the unexpected presence of Jesus, the answer to some unasked question.

She molds the sand patiently, her hands just starting to show the beginnings of veiny wrinkles. We are both looking for God. We could not be more alike; we could not be more different.

In the wake of the unexpected wave, everything is drenched

and cool. Dane, too, has stripped off his bathing suit now and is running back and forth in the water in Superman underwear. *Low tide.*

I walk toward the kids, thinking about the tide, the daily pull of it, the way the ocean lets herself be moved. I have spent a lot of my life waiting for God to show up like a tidal wave, sudden and shattering and overwhelming. And for a while he did. But then he did less, and I started to think it was because of me. That I'd lost some essential way of faith.

But the ocean is at low tide now, and this is not her failing but simply the rhythms of life.

I wander slowly toward Dane and Liam—silhouettes of darkness against a curtain of light. As I walk, I can feel the weight of this journey—1,720.2 miles, give or take—and of my own inertia. My wintering faith.

I wonder what would happen if I learned to accept these silent rhythms as a normal part of faith: *light and dark, high tide and low tide, summer and winter.* What if I stopped fighting, stopped going crazy trying to fill in the gap, stopped running?

What would it look like to give in to these rhythms? What if I learned to love my heavy heart? To stop scrambling to *be in the light.* What if instead I let God pull me lower and lower, like the moon pulls the sea?

Would I drown? Would I rise?

I have to holler at the kids five times before they finally come running, soaked and smiling, sand in their eyelashes gleaming like gold. "Come here! Come see this sand castle that Miss Donna made for you!"

The kids fly past me and slide to their knees at the piles that Donna has made as she points out towers and turrets, and I think about photographs I've seen—single sand grains magnified until they look like stars, like entire universes of their own. I think about the ocean, how the light penetrates only the first two hundred meters. How the deeper you go, the darker it gets.

There is so much that I don't understand.

The tide is low, and the beach is expansive in its beauty, infinite in incomprehensible treasures, big as the entire world, small as a grain of sand. And God is like fire and like rain. Like high tide and low tide and everything in between. He is a wave rushing in and like the moon pulling the sea out. He is here—even in the empty, endless white of the sky, even in the deepest dark of the ocean.

"Now," Donna says. "I want you to wreck it."

"*Wreck it?*" Dane asks, his eyes wide, equal parts excitement and horror.

"Yes! That's the best part!" Donna says, laughing that rough smoker's laugh. "On the count of one . . . two . . . THREE!"

Donna laughs and claps as Dane and Liam dinosaur-stomp the sand castle smooth.

"Okay, guys. Say good-bye!" I tell the kids, and they wave to Donna as we turn and head toward the parking lot. "Have a great birthday!" I call out as we tromp up the beach.

"Have a great trip home!" She picks up her damp Bible and clutches it close to her beating heart. She waves and waves and waves until we're gone.

The boys are dripping wet, and so are the borrowed bath towels that were in my blue-striped beach bag. We are sand-caked and sunburned and tired and happy. We hoof it up the wooden steps into the parking lot. I strip them down one at a time—first Liam, then Dane. I wipe them down the best I can and then help them into some mismatched dry clothes knocked loose from my tote-bag system and drifting around in the van.

I back out of the parking lot and away from the Florida shore-line for the last time. In the rearview mirror, I can see the sun and the water and the dark, straight hair of a woman meeting her God at the ocean. And in the end I suppose it doesn't matter why you come to the roaring edge of the world. Maybe it doesn't even really matter what you find there. Maybe all that matters is that you come.

Part IV

||||||

I will learn,
I will learn to love the skies I'm under.

—Mumford & Sons,
"Hopeless Wanderer"

Ormond Beach, Florida, to Savannah, Georgia

Monday, February 24, 2014

On Monday morning we leave Florida. The traffic is horrendous. I-95 filled, I suppose, with commuters getting about their week. I can't see the ocean anymore as we creep along the stopped-up highway, bearing north.

Yesterday afternoon, after the beach, I brought in every last scrap of our dirty laundry and took over Julie's washer and dryer for most of the day. Basket by basket I dumped the clean clothes into the middle of the guest bed and set about refolding them into totes for our next stretch of overnight stops. *Savannah. North Carolina. Louisville. Chicago.* Each folded fleece hoodie felt like a signpost pointing me back to Minnesota winter, and I felt myself bracing for it even then, in the light-flooded guest bedroom of Josh and Julie's Florida home.

This morning was a flurry of gathering our things, of packing and repacking the car, of picking up stale french fries and loose granola-bar wrappers off the sand-and-cracker-crumb-coated floor of the van and throwing them away. By the time we'd given our hugs, said our good-byes, and coasted out of the driveway waving madly at Julie and her family, I was already exhausted.

I turn the music on and sip at my gas-station coffee, which I bought at the Ormond Beach Texaco before we got on the highway. It's become a ritual of our trip—these gas-station breakfasts, cobbled together in the car. The coffee's a little lukewarm, and the muffin I bought has left crumbles all over my floor and mashed bits of chocolate on my blue jeans. Dane lobs a half-empty bag of prepackaged fruit at me, and a grape bounces off the dash. "Here, Mom," he says distractedly. "I'm done."

It's official: we're on the road again.

Billboards advertise the Florida Citrus Center. WIND CHIMES! 13-FOOT GATOR! FREE ORANGE JUICE! DISNEY SOUVENIRS! The billboards are making one last grasp for your money. *How will you remember that you were here if you don't have proof?* the signs seem to say. *Buy a postcard! A seashell jewelry box! A gator head!*

But we don't. We move onward up the coast, close enough to the ocean that I can almost feel the tug of it. The phone rings, and I jump a little. When I answer it, I hear Andrew's voice on the line.

"Hey, sweets!"

"Hey! Can you hear me?"

"Yes!" Yesterday after the incident with the ocean, the borrowed phone had seemed fine—except for the speaker. When I'd tried to call Andrew that afternoon, I'd been able to hear him, but he couldn't hear me. After a couple of unsuccessful attempts, I'd given up and buried my face in the guest-room pillow to scream for ten minutes before walking calmly downstairs and asking Julie for a small plastic bag of rice.

"You can? You can really hear me?!"

"I can hear you, Presh!"

"Hooray! It's a Road Trip Miracle!"

"What's a miracle, Mom?" Dane asks from behind me.

"So you're on the road, then?" Andrew asks.

"WHAT MIRACLE, MOM?!" Dane shouts, louder.

I turn back toward him. "Just that Mommy's phone is working."

"Oh," he says, satisfied, and returns to his movie. By now he's gotten used to prayers that involve dead phones.

"Yeah, we're on the road. We just left maybe forty-five minutes ago? We should be to Savannah by lunchtime. I'm taking them to that restaurant with all the baby alligators."

"Oh, yeah. I remember you showing me that. Seventy gators?"

"Seventy-eight, apparently."

"Wowzer."

"I know. They're going to be *jazzed*."

Savannah is the only stop on the whole road trip where I've planned for a hotel instead of looking for a friend or an acquaintance with whom to stay. There will be no reading gig at some church or bookshop, no meet-ups with strangers, no small talk of any kind. Just me and the kids. It feels like exactly what we all need.

The road curves down a thin, two-lane road lined with marshlands toward the tiny beach town of Tybee Island. Our Crab Shack stop is short and sweet and just a bit out of the way. The restaurant is sparsely populated by customers during this off-season Monday lunch hour, but it's fully populated with baby gators. We stay for an hour or so, watching them loll in the weak winter sunlight, lazily making their way across the blue-dyed "lagoon." Then we get back into the car and eat Aldi-brand potato chips and granola bars for lunch and continue into the tiny, tourist town of Tybee.

Tybee Island is all but deserted, a ghost town full of closed gift shops and rental places, shoddy brick hotels with green-blinking Vacancy signs and off-season sales. When we pull into the beach parking lot, we find that it's empty, too.

"We're here!" I say to the kids.

"What are we doin'?" Dane wants to know, tossing his empty chip bag toward the trash bag and missing.

"We're going to check out another beach. Maybe we can find some more shells."

"Okay!" Dane says, eager to add to his collection. He unbuckles and jumps up.

"Beach!" Liam shouts, eager to get out of the car. "Help!" He reaches his arms out and flails them in the air until I open his car door, unlatch his five-point harness, and let him down onto the sidewalk.

The cattails look lonely and chilled, slanting up from among the sand dunes. The ocean air is cold against our skin as we stand in the parking lot getting ready. I feed the meter and put the boys in sweatshirts. We leave our shoes beside the dunes and then head for the shoreline. Even though the temperatures are low here and the wind is brisk, Dane and Liam run toward the water, screaming when the cold waves lick their feet.

I sit down on the sand and wrap my arms around my legs. Across the ocean shallows, wintering shorebirds swoop and dive. I don't know enough about birds to know which type they are. Andrew would know—he loves birds. As for me, all I can tell is that they're white and gull-like with ink-dipped wings. I don't know if they're native to this place or if they've come a long way to be here, but I like to think they're from somewhere cold and distant—like us. That they—that we—have all somehow earned a moment or two of airborne joy in exchange for the journey we made to get here.

There is a certain mystery to migration that amazes me—the way birds know when to lift off the half-frozen earth and fly. The way they flock in perfectly arranged configurations at sunset and then navigate, somehow by stars and sense, by the pull of the magnetic earth, by a compass in their beating hearts, by a map imprinted on their hollow bones.

I feel a certain kinship to the snowbirds. It makes sense to me—the impulse to migrate. The days get shorter and life gets darker, and the circadian rhythms of my heart swing off-kilter, and I feel that drive, too, to *go*. After all, I belong to the generation of the restless and rootless. We're not sure where we're going, but we'll know it when we see it—this elusive place of plenty. It's anywhere but *here*. So we're winging through the wide-open night, trying to find true north from the rotational star pattern, constantly distracted by the glimmering of artificial light of very tall buildings and very bright cities.

We get blown off course. We become lost.

We keep looking.

I watch Dane and Liam in their shorts and hooded sweatshirts, their hair soft and windswept. They're standing as still as I've seen them all day—all week, maybe all *year*—staring out toward the horizon, shivering slightly. Dane bends down and begins to draw designs in the packed wet sand, lines linking circles. "Look at my map, Mom!" he yells.

I stand up and brush off my jeans and walk to the shore. "That's so cool, buddy," I tell him, and he beams up at me.

Around us the shorebirds are diving and the ocean is beating against our toes. Back at home, where we're headed, the snow is falling, falling, falling, burying the world all over again. The pond in our backyard is blanketed in thick, snow-pocked ice, and I can picture it perfectly, even as I stand here: the frozen water surrounded by the bulky suburban homes. The bare branches of maples and oaks. The hearty pine. The deck, buried in snow, dotted with frozen bits of dog poop, indented with pee, since Marty won't go down the stairs when it's this cold. The swing set, half buried and still in the quiet cold.

And *birds*.

I'd forgotten about the birds.

In the middle of the subzero temperatures and the long winter nights, they're still there. The blue jay, proud and imposing, winging around the yard, chasing away the smaller birds, arcing back under the chilled sky. She could migrate—some blue jays do. But the one in our yard stays, every winter, resting in the shivering branches, landing on the snow-covered banister of the deck, waiting.

The chickadee is fluttering circles around her, moving through the bald branches of the lilac bush when most of the other birds have gone away. She knows how to lower her body temperature and to find caches of stored food. She is unafraid, this tiny bird with her black hat and slate-gray back and tail. They say if you're very still, she will hop up and eat right out of your hand.

And maybe I'm a snowbird—or maybe I'm not. Maybe all this ever was was a case of mistaken identity. I thought I needed to fly away to survive. I'd forgotten about the simple ways we are saved exactly where we are.

The kids start running in circles, up and down the beach, laughing as they go, and the birds arc above us. The wind is whipping around us, ruffling the feathers of the birds, lifting my hair off my neck, and I feel strong. I am light-boned and scrappy. Solid and beloved.

It may just turn out that I am built for survival.

Our room at the Inn at Ellis Square in Savannah is so small that I can barely fit the double stroller inside. I booked the hotel because Julie had raved. "It's so *Savannah*," she'd said as we sat on her couch in Florida. "Beautiful woodwork and high ceilings and right on the river. You'll love it." I jam the stroller between the TV stand and the vanity and open the curtains. Admittedly, there is a stunning view of the Savannah River, but it's a little hard to appreciate it with Dane and Liam jumping back and forth between the two queen beds. "Superman!" Dane shouts.

"Minja Turtle power!" Liam replies. I remember that Julie's stay at the Inn at Ellis Square had been for a wedding she was shooting. *Sans kids.* Which suddenly explains so much.

"Hey, you crazies," I say, pulling on a sweatshirt and jeans. "Let's go explore!"

"YEAH!" they shout, and I can't understand their boundless energy—some fountain that just keeps recycling itself in an unending stream of insanity. I'm so tired I feel like I could fall over.

The hotel is just around the corner from the famous Savannah City Market, so I push the stroller there, and we walk. We admire the colorful wind socks hanging from arched shop doorways and old wooden wagons with red metal wheels. For a long time, we linger at a fountain at the center of the square, where the water shoots up in straight jets—crystalline bars of water and sunlight. Dane and Liam get close to the spray and then retreat, laughing maniacally. A lone goateed musician is playing a guitar to an empty restaurant patio nearby, and I can hear the hopeful sound of his voice mingle with the rush of the fountain and the muffled voices of southern strangers on their cell phones. *Savannah.*

When the kids are hungry, we stop for dinner at Vinnie Van GoGo's, a little pizza place at the very end of the market. Our table faces the market square, and behind us, through the window, we can see bearded young hipsters slinging dough into pizza rounds on the tips of their fingers.

While we wait, I take out a small bag of plastic toy animals from my purse, and we play with them together at the table. I order a glass of wine—sauvignon blanc—the cheapest glass on the menu. It comes in a plastic cup, and when I sip it slowly alongside the pizza, it tastes, for the first time in a long time, like it's supposed to. Not medicinal but miraculous. Cheap grapes crushed, fermented, sipped slowly, carefully, gratefully.

And it could be the play of light through the trees or the sound of the wind socks whistling. It could be the way Dane looks at me when he makes his toy rhinoceros talk to my toy hippo. But for some reason, in the setting light of the Savannah day, the pizza crust that Liam hands me—"You eat"—feels like *Body of Christ, broken for you,* the wine feels like *Blood of Christ, shed for you,* and I feel like this small meal in the evening glow of Savannah is making me whole.

"Here, Mom," Dane says. "You can have my crust, too."

"Thanks!" I tell them. "Hippo *loves* crusts." Their laugh comes in sweet bubbles, light like my sauvignon blanc, and it's cobbled-together road-trip Communion all over again. It's exactly what I need . . . the only way I can take it. And so I do. I take. Eat. Drink.

Remember.

When we've finished, the kids clamber into the stroller with their cups of pink lemonade and we begin, again, to walk.

Our old garage-sale double stroller is bulky and stubborn and nearly impossible to push uphill with both boys inside. I have to ask Dane to get out when I'm trying to get up over the curbs, and he obliges, helping to tug the front of the stroller over the ragged concrete curbs. Standing there in his gray track pants and green hoodie sweatshirt, he looks so big—a million miles from that splotchy-faced baby who changed everything all those years ago. He waits for me to resituate the stroller, which rattles and groans as if it just might collapse into pieces in the middle of Savannah, and then he climbs back in.

Around us the evening light is slowly fading into the branches of stately old trees. I'm not sure where I'm going or how far to walk before I turn around. I know almost nothing about this city, but it folds over us like a shelter. We keep coming across lovely stone fountains, surrounded by benches and the low-bent branches of willows. We stop to throw pennies every time we see one, leaving secret wishes at the bottom of a half dozen clear pools in this quiet pocket of the South.

By the time we get to the grand design school at the top of the hill and turn around, it's officially dark. The kids are quiet and heavy in the stroller, and I have to lean in to the weight as we walk. The brew houses and restaurants are lit up now from within, and I can see the young professionals laughing at bars and around tables, lifting local food to their mouths. To our right, storefronts display a hundred beautiful things under low spotlights—ruffled dresses fitted to curvy mannequins, chevron-patterned dishes, leather messenger bags, bulky, glittering jewelry.

It occurs to me as we cross Bay Street in the glow of the waiting headlights of cars that this is the first time I've been out at night on this trip. I've been to the van, of course, in transit to or from speaking engagements or to the next house where we were meant to stay. I've been in the driveways of people's homes, gathering things into the laundry basket for the night, looking up for one breathless moment at the sky. But I haven't been *out* out. In the street, wandering, letting the warm dark settle around me.

It's beautiful.

On the other side of Bay Street, a valet opens the door to a restaurant and directs us to take the elevator down to the first floor to get to the riverfront. I thank him and shove the stroller into the marble halls and then into the elevator, where the kids are wide-eyed in the spotless mirrors. On the first floor, I have to heave the old rickety thing through a swanky bar, where waiters in crisp white shirts walk by with trays of cocktails and thin women in little black dresses lean across tables laughing.

I'm wearing the same jeans that I had on when we left Julie's house this morning—coffee-stained in more than a few spots—and a hoodie. My hair, once curling prettily down my back, is now a wild bramble, not all that unlike the marshlands we passed on our way to Tybee Island this morning.

We walk through the restaurant, looking like impostors, and then out the back door onto River Street, where the bright lights of the restaurants on one side of the road sit in stark contrast to the dark, silent river on the other.

"Hey, pretty lady." Another valet—younger—waves to me from the front of a swanky-looking restaurant. He is short and dark-skinned and undeniably handsome, and I smile and give him a small wave. "Where y'all from?" he wants to know.

I'm flattered. I'm baffled. I wonder if he can see the bulky stroller full of kids that I'm pushing across the sidewalk.

If I answer him, I know what will happen. There will be the telltale electric bolt of excitement that comes from this kind of attention. I know the feel of it, the glittering glow of it. It's sparkly and smooth—this flirtation—a pretty stone that I'd like to grab, stick in my pocket, keep for a day down the road when I might need to take it out and look at it again.

I could idle here for a minute and rock the stroller back and forth, talk to the guy, flip my hair, let the jolt of attention pull me out of the numb exhaustion of so many miles. It would look harmless to any passerby—just an innocent conversation, just a harmless dalliance with a handsome younger man, who for some reason is looking at me like I just stepped out of a magazine instead of a minivan.

There is a part of me that wants to stay.

But more than that, I want to go to the river. I want to stand next to the dark water. I want to see what's waiting for us there.

"Where's your man tonight?" The handsome valet tries again, eyeing the ring on my finger. He's young. Cocky. His smile stretches wide and dimpled across his smooth face. "If I had a beautiful lady like you, I'd sure be with her on a night like tonight!"

The contour of his accent is smooth like red wine, and I could get drunk on it if I wanted to.

But I don't.

"He's home," I say. "Waiting for us." I give one last little wave and turn to cross the street. I don't look back as I push the heavy stroller toward the obsidian surface of the river—not even for one wistful moment. And for the first time in almost two thousand miles, I feel like the brave woman that everyone keeps telling me I am.

The cables on the Talmadge Memorial Bridge glow white as they angle up into two graceful triangles, spanning nearly two miles across the Savannah River. The docked boats are still and quiet, and even the river's flow seems to have hushed.

Beside the water, hemmed in by shadow, an old man plays his saxophone. I take a dollar from my purse and hand it to Dane. "Go give this to that guy playing," I tell him quietly.

"Come *with* me," he begs.

"You can do it," I tell him. "You are *brave*."

"I am?"

"You are."

He hesitates a moment, then pulls himself out of the stroller and walks tentatively toward the man. He stands for one undecided moment, and then he reaches over to put the dollar in the saxophone case.

"Well, thanks, little man!" the musician says, his voice rough with joy. Under his driver's cap, the stranger's smile gleams big and bright and sincere. "So. What you wanna hear? 'Hokey Pokey' or 'Twinkle, Twinkle'?"

I can't hear Dane's answer, but a moment later he's back in the stroller and the man is playing "Twinkle, Twinkle, Little Star." The saxophone riffs on the familiar ditty, its mournful cry sliding up and down the melody. The boys sit in the stroller, motionless, watching.

Tonight the moon is a waning crescent, 31 percent visible—a picturesque, nursery-rhyme kind of moon. By tomorrow it will be a scrap, then a sliver, then barely anything at all—just a phantom glow in the sky.

We left Minnesota at the height of the full moon. I drove into Wisconsin, and it was pregnant with light, glowing under the darkness, turning the night sky blue. It has been waning ever since, every night a little less visible, only one-tenth as bright today as it was the night we left. Every day that I have been driving madly toward the Light, the night has gotten imperceptibly darker.

And yet.

Twinkle, twinkle, little star, the saxophone calls, and I feel myself expand into the hospitality of this music, this darkness. When the musician finishes, we clap, and he grins at us again— "Thank ya! Thank y'all very much!"—and begins packing up his instrument. We wave and turn around, heading toward the end of the river path, where I let the boys out of the stroller. I sit on the grass on the bank of the river, while they wander around the empty path, looking for trash and treasures by the dim light of the streetlamps.

The city lights play along the surface of the water, and a flock of birds flies overhead. You would miss them entirely but for how the bridge's light sparks against their spread wings.

I think about the ways I have spent most of my life confusing the natural waning of light with a dying faith. *Low tide. Fading moon. Shortening days. Dormant trees. Migrating birds, flying away.* The truth is perhaps simpler than that. Maybe none of this is a kind of failure—just a turning of seasons, the cyclical movement of time.

Is it possible that I don't need as much light as I always thought I did?

As I look at the river, my eyes begin to adjust, and I can see the dark texture of the water, the glowing blades of grass, the bending branches of the trees. All of it beautiful.

I sit there like that for a few minutes. The minutes feel like an ellipsis, a tentative bridge, the indefinable *Selah* between the verses of a psalm. Then Liam climbs heavily into the back of the stroller and crosses his arms. "You ready to go, buddy?" I ask, and he gives me one sharp nod, his lips pursed into a pout. His gray sweatshirt has come partway unzipped, and I can see the red lizard T-shirt underneath, speckled with pizza sauce.

"All right, then," I say, kicking the brake pedal up and shoving the stroller into motion. "Let's do it."

Savannah, Georgia, to
Charlotte, North Carolina

Tuesday, February 25, 2014

The next morning we cross the bridge out of Savannah and toward South Carolina. A few miles past the state line, we spy two giant fake elephants—one pink, one gray.

They stand, an odd lonely pair, in the empty gravel parking lot of Papa Joe's Fireworks. "Elephants!" Liam shouts from behind me. He's put his Ninja Turtle cap on backward and is pointing frantically out the window. "Elephants! Elephants!"

"Wow!" Dane adds when he looks out Liam's window and sees the elephants, too. "Stop the car, Mom!"

There is no particular reason to stop. But there's also no reason not to. So I make a sharp turn into the lot and park in the middle. The boys tumble out of the van and run for the elephants, ducking underneath wide, wrinkled legs, hanging from arching plastic trunks, and it's only taken me two thousand–ish miles, but I've finally achieved at least one kitschy, roadside victory. *Huzzah.*

My plan for today had been to make a long lunch stop in Charleston, South Carolina, before heading up to Charlotte for one last reading on the cobbled-together "book tour" portion of the road trip. I liked the idea of Charleston—ocean and architecture and rich cultural threads weaving into something unique. I thought that I would show the kids the sailboats coming in and out of the harbor as we sat among the palmetto trees. I thought they'd maybe play in the Pineapple Fountain. I thought I might try gumbo.

But last night I'd sat cross-legged and exhausted on the hotel bed after our river walk, studying the map, counting out hours on my fingers. *Savannah to Charleston, Charleston to Charlotte.* No matter how many times I did the math, the numbers didn't add up.

The familiar, soft hymn-lullabies played on a loop on the iHome that I'd set on the TV stand. The kids had fallen asleep twenty minutes before, but I didn't have the energy to get up and turn the music off. They lay, turned toward each other, under the white hotel duvet in a pool of spilled light from the open bathroom. As I looked at them, the three-hour detour seemed not only logically impossible but also cruel. I could tell that we were, all of us, running out of steam, losing momentum, getting low on that old adventuring spirit.

So this morning when we'd left the Inn at Ellis Square, we'd slanted west toward the nondescript center of South Carolina instead of north along her famous coast. We wound our way out of the hotel parking ramp and into the sun-dappled city morning. In Dane's lap a bowl of Styrofoam remains of plates and bowls that he methodically ripped up during the hotel continental breakfast instead of eating his toast. "They're my tickets, Mom!" he'd insisted, and I'd shaken my head and taken another sip of coffee.

U.S. 17 took us out of town, up the steep slope of the Talmadge Memorial Bridge with its taut white cables bisecting the bright blue sky. It took us over the smooth back of the river and to these giant elephant statues, where we are now idling, happily ensconced in roadside silliness.

"Take a picture of me by the elephant, Mom!" Dane shouts, and I do.

I snap photos of my children with my borrowed iPhone. They're swinging from elephant trunks and laughing at the elephant butts with their still-hanging tails. "Butt!" Liam says. "Butt, butt, butt!" and Dane doubles over, laughing. "Eww!" *Click, click, click, click.* I take one photo after another until they've exhausted the possibilities of the elephants and we're all strapped back into the car.

I drive north on I-95. The trees alongside the road are beginning to thin just a little. Gone are the waving palms of Florida and the pink-and-white magnolia blooms of Georgia. We're still in T-shirts, but the shorts are packed away now, stashed into tote bags, stuffed into the back of the van. I can feel the landscape changing around us, the tiniest threads of winter beginning to reach toward us across state lines.

In my audiobook Mamah and Frank are driving, too—up a gravel road in Wisconsin to the spot where Frank has built his architectural masterpiece—Taliesin. A house nestled into a hill, modern and isolated and like nothing else in the world—"a great golden vista." It's hard to say whether Mamah wants to be there or not. I get the sense that her heart is still in Europe. But she follows Frank nevertheless into his half-finished dream home, where she will spend the rest of her life.

Beyond the doors of Taliesin, reporters are camped out, trying to get a whiff of a story. The locals know that Mamah is mistress, not wife, and are less than friendly—and Frank's family lives just down the road. Whatever sense of self Mamah found in Europe has been subjugated now to the daily work of running a home, to making meals for Taliesin's construction crew, to living the domesticated Wisconsin life. At the kitchen table, Frank's mother subtly criticizes her cooking.

To make things worse, it's turning out that Frank is terrible with money—in debt to all sorts of people and recklessly filling their house with grand furniture. And he won't let her plant flowers because it messes with his artistic vision. "Bet you wish you'd stayed with the other guy, huh?" I say to the CD player. "At least you could have had a garden."

"What, Mom?"

"Nothing."

At the tip-top of South Carolina, I turn off the highway and begin to weave through the winding back roads, where big, sheltering trees bow low over the road and the light comes broken through the branches. Tonight we're staying with a woman I've never met—a reader of my blog and a new e-mail friend. Debbie and her husband, Rob, are empty-nesters, and when I'd decided to drive home by way of the East Coast, she'd offered us a room at their farmhouse outside Charlotte. "We have a horse, and the boys can feed him carrots," she'd said in an e-mail. "Sold," I'd replied.

Now I pull onto the gravel road that loops into the pristine, picturesque farm and feel my mouth drop open. Behind the slanting eaves of the classic farmhouse, there is a classic red barn and a handsome brown horse. An apple tree in the yard has just barely started to bloom, and there are little flurries of pink flowers on all the branches. It feels like I've driven onto the set of a movie.

Debbie is petite, with short blond hair. Glasses. Kind eyes. She has a matter-of-fact way of speaking, a little gravelly, tinged with a southern drawl. "Hey, boys!" she says as the kids tumble onto the grass, blinking around at the wide-open space while I crawl around in the backseat looking for their socks. "I don't suppose you wanna see a horse?" Her tall, gray-haired husband, Rob, smiles softly at us from behind the fence posts, and two little dogs yip around at his feet. "Welcome," he says, giving me a tentative hug. And just like that, it's as if we're home.

I have a book reading scheduled that night at Debbie and Rob's church in Charlotte, and the group is already settled into rows of chairs in the church's front room when we get there. They're drinking coffee from an assortment of mugs, waiting patiently, talking softly, when we finally burst through the doors. Late. Again.

I hurry the boys into the nursery, and blessedly, they go without a fight. Rob carries my box of books to the back table, and Debbie gives me coffee. A young pastor introduces me with kind words that sound like static to my frenzied mind, and then I'm standing there, book in one hand, mug in the other, feeling flustered and unprepared.

But when I start reading from the book, the people in front of me look at me so kindly, nod so gently. The willowy-haired and wrinkled and the young and smooth-faced. They span the whole spectrum, and they have all *been there*—to the dark bottom of faith—each of them in his or her own particular way. I can't explain how I know this—I just sense it rivering between us all in the windowed front room. My breathing begins to even out, and I stop clinging to my coffee mug for dear life.

When I'm done reading, we open it up for questions, and a young guy in ironic glasses and skinny jeans asks about my drinking. "I appreciated your honesty in your book when you talked about your drinking. Could you talk a little about your relationship with alcohol now?"

I lift the coffee cup to my lips and pretend that I am calmly considering this instead of panicking. Is it possible that this guy saw me last week when I was downing miniature bottles of cabernet in Julie's driveway?

When I finally swallow the coffee over the giant lump of dread in my mouth, I tell him that I have not turned out to be an alcoholic. At least not yet. I don't go into the specifics of why I believe this. I don't tell this audience that I am always watching for it. That I am aware that there is a *line* somewhere and that if I cross that line, everything will change. I have read enough memoirs, watched enough movies, listened to enough stories to know that if I do, that glass of wine will no longer be about giving me a little lift—but rather about keeping me alive, even as it's killing me. And I don't want that.

"I'm still trying to figure out how to have a healthy relationship with alcohol," I say. "Like many kids who grew up in this version of Christianity, I spent a lot of my life pinging between absolutes. Black and white. Good and evil. I'm still trying to figure out the gray. The middle ground. The moderation thing." A couple of people chuckle, and I take a sip of my coffee.

Of course, this is only part of the truth about me and booze. The other part has to do with the darkness that I'm always trying to escape—and that, for me, the hardest part of my journey with alcohol is not really controlling the *amount*—though obviously that's a factor. The hardest part for me has to do with motives. With learning to drink toward communion, not oblivion. Drinking a glass of wine while I confront the pain head-on with a friend, rather than a whole bottle, alone, to anesthetize it. Drinking to savor the moment, to celebrate, to let the world in—this is what I'm still trying to learn.

Like all beautiful things, wine is a little bit dangerous. Which perhaps is why Jesus chose it as the metaphor of his love when he said, *Take, drink. Do this in remembrance of me.*

"What's next?" someone asks toward the end of the talk, and it's a moment before I realize we're not still talking about drinking. "What will your next book be about?"

I falter, trying to string together stray thoughts into something solid. Ultimately I trail off and shrug. "I guess I don't really know."

The audience nods graciously and moves on, but I can't shake the question. *What's next?* I think as I shake hands, sign books, try unsuccessfully to log in to my Square credit-card reader with my cousin's borrowed phone.

What comes after you've taken that first wobbly step back to faith, to church, to God? What happens after you've chosen to forgive—both *them* and *yourself*—but the actual work of it feels so endless that you don't know where to start? What's next after you've driven 1,702.2 miles to the ocean and then turned the van back around? After you've sat in the many-layered beauty of the darkness? After you've finally taken a second to *look at it,* to breathe it in?

Dane and Liam come running into the room alongside the pastor's children. The audience is beginning to trickle out now—kindred strangers. Church People. I watch them go, my book tucked under their arms, chatting as they walk across the dark parking lot. They pull their coats tight around themselves in the shadows of the streetlights, bracing themselves against the sharp end of the southern winter.

Then there are just a handful of us left. Rob and Debbie—who spent the last twenty minutes on the phone outside the front doors and now looks drawn and stressed—and also a young couple I know from the Internet. They are tall and beautiful, chatting and laughing in the emptying room. But underneath their easy smiles, their marriage imperceptibly dissolving beneath them. By this time next year, they'll be separated, in counseling, trying to figure out the answer to that very same question: *What's next?* What's next when the bottom falls out? What's next after the wrecking ball has broken against your life and it's time to get up and move forward. *What's next?*

We turn out the lights and head to the parking lot. The moon is less than a quarter of itself, but you can see the shadow of wholeness—the ghost silhouette of a full, round moon held in the heart of this emptiness. The boys are shivering a little when I put them into their car seats, start a DVD, crank up the heat.

We stand outside the cars and chat until it's too cold and we're too tired, and then I get into the van and follow Rob and Debbie back to their farm. I've driven thousands of miles, spent hours and hours searching for God, and I suppose what's next is learning what it means to go home.

It's late when we get back from the reading. I thought the kids might fall asleep in the car, but they stayed awake the whole time, blinking at an episode of *Curious George* on the dual monitors of the car DVD player.

Back at the farmhouse, I put them both into the double bed in the room of one of Debbie and Rob's daughters. A big wooden hutch full of pretty things dominates the wall, and moonlight streams in through the window.

The bed is tall, and they are tiny in it. "Lay with us, Mom," Dane says drowsily, and I do. I turn on the lullabies, and we lie still while the lilting words of an old hymn fill the room with cello and viola, melody and piano and harmonies. It was written in the 1800s by a blind housewife named Mrs. C. H. Morris and covered by a group called Page CXVI. The old hymn makes me want to cry as I rest my forehead against Dane's and curl my arms around him. On the other side, Liam's already fast asleep.

> *Nearer, still nearer, close to Thy heart.*
> *Draw me, dear Savior, precious thou art.*

"I miss my room, Mom." Dane sighs. "And Dad and Marty. And my door."

> *And fold me, oh, fold me, close to Thy breast.*
> *Shelter me safe in your Haven of Rest.*

"I know, buddy," I breathe, pulling him closer. "Just a couple more days and we'll be home."

I squeeze him tighter and hold him against me. His hair is soft and damp with sweat. He smells like french fries and cookie crumbs and strawberries and hope. I rest my head against his until his breath evens out and his eyes begin to flicker beneath closed lids and he's asleep.

Slowly I uncurl myself and pad downstairs to the kitchen in my sweatpants, sweatshirt, and socks, to talk to my hosts.

Rob and Debbie are sitting in the dark dining room at the computer desk by the wall, looking for flights to New Orleans. The only illumination in the room is a low oven light and the computer fluorescence, reflecting the blues of airline ads onto Debbie's tired face. She looks like she's aged five years since we pulled into the driveway, her mouth pinched with concern, her own worry line creased deep into her forehead.

I feel like I'm intruding, but Rob smiles and says, "Sit down, sit down." He pours me a glass of water, and I sit curled up at the table, waiting.

"This would get me there on Wednesday at . . . fiveish and put me back here on Sunday," she says, and whether she's talking to Rob or to herself, I can't tell. "I don't know."

She sits a minute, her hand hesitating over the computer mouse, before shaking her head and closing the window. "I need to think," she says, looking at Rob. "I can't do this right now."

"Sorry," she says looking at me. She takes off her glasses and rubs her eyes.

"Don't worry about it at all. Is everything okay?" I ask, knowing already that it's not.

"Our oldest daughter, Anna." She sighs, looking at Rob. "She's had a rough year, and she left me a message during your reading. She's really struggling in law school. . . ." Debbie trails off, and though she doesn't explain much more about it, I can feel the weight of all that is unspoken.

It's just one part of a long, hard story that Rob and Debbie begin to tell me. The story begins more than a decade ago with a fluke car accident—Debbie and her daughters sitting at a stop sign when the girls are young. Out of nowhere the crash of metal and steel. An instant. A lifetime.

Debbie and Anna sustained only minor injuries, but her younger daughter, Evie, spent months in the hospital with major trauma to the head. They tell me that while she recovered, she'll always have seizures, that Debbie spends a lot of time with her in various doctors' offices and hospital rooms, trying to get meds straightened out and dosages adjusted. Evie bears the marks of that day on her forever, and so do her parents.

"She had just picked out a Bible," Debbie recalls. "She'd begged for it at the store, and she was so happy sitting there with it."

"She was holding it on her lap when they got hit," Rob adds. "Brand-new Bible. So proud."

In the wake of the accident, life went on. The older daughter, Anna, went off to college and then law school, where she met a man who became her best friend. Then her boyfriend. And then, one year ago, just a few days before Mardi Gras, he was killed. Another car accident, another collision, another moment that changes the whole damn thing.

Debbie talks, and Rob interjects every now and then, adding a detail from where he stands, leaning against the counter with a glass of water in his hand. It's a story they've told before, a story that has marked how their family has seen the world. A story that has made Debbie and Rob cling desperately to God, a story that has pushed Anna away from him.

I keep picturing their young daughter strapped into the back-seat of the car. It's nothing like my story, and it would be insensitive and false of me to equate my pain to hers. But also, on some level, it makes sense to me. It *feels* familiar: One minute you're holding your Bible—so sure, so proud—and the next minute something crashes into you. And everything changes.

In the dark kitchen, I feel as if my eyes are finally beginning to adjust. And I'd forgotten that this is how sight works. We move from someplace *very bright* to someplace *very dark,* and for several minutes it's very hard to see. But then the pupil expands and the rod cells engage, and the whole eye is flooded with rhodopsin, and we can finally absorb photos, perceive light. I'd forgotten that we are *made like this.* We are equipped to see not only in the light . . . but also in the darkness. It just takes time to switch between the two.

And maybe this has all been nothing more than part of the natural process of things. I spent the formative years of my life, my faith, looking straight into the Light. It only makes sense that it would take my eyes a while to heal from that burning and to adjust to a world that so often is dark. But now I'm sitting at the kitchen table, blinking in the darkness, and God's presence doesn't feel at all like fog lights or romance or smoke or fire. It is as steady and commonplace as the wooden farm table between us, the floor my feet brush against, the slant of the oven light barely illuminating the table. It's almost pitch-black. I've never seen so clearly.

Debbie and Rob are not touching, but their bodies seem to be oriented toward each other—leaning on each other in the telling.

There is no wine bottle open on the table, no anesthetizing this with booze, no flipping on artificial lights to dispel the pain with easy answers. Here at Debbie and Rob's kitchen table, there can be no attempt to fix the darkness or to hide from it, no igniting it with a strobe of contrived emotion. There is only surrender to the God who resurrects, who makes new—and who does this work so often in the darkest of places. The belly of a whale, the midnight quiet of a garden, the rock-closed tomb.

I sit very still at the table. And what the darkness asks of me is different from what the light does. In the darkness I am asked to listen. To wait. To allow myself to be folded close to the heart of God. It is good in a way that terrifies me. It is the other side of hospitality—and I am not the one with anything to offer here.

I sit with Rob and Debbie until there is nothing left to say, nothing left to hear, only the buzzing of the refrigerator, the soft padding of the dogs' paws against the wooden floor.

Later I'll be reading the first chapter of Genesis, and I'll think of this moment. For the first time, I'll notice the verses that come before the famous creation narrative begins to unfold. Before God starts the whole thing off with those powerful, bellowing words— *"Let there be light!"* Before he calls it *good* and separates it out from the darkness . . . *before that* there is nothing—just the Holy Spirit hovering in the formless void. Just God and the darkness that covers the surface of the deep.

Just nothing. Just everything.

Then we say good night and I climb the stairs to the guest room at the end of the hall. The walls are covered with the leftover miscellany of a high-school girl who carried her own heavy things out of this house and into the world.

I lie down on the tall poster bed, turn out the lamp, and let myself drift to sleep in the hospitable, layered silence of God.

Charlotte, North Carolina, to Buffalo Grove, Illinois

Wednesday, February 26, to Thursday, February 27, 2014

On the way out of Charlotte the next morning, I miss the exit at least four times, maybe five. For nearly twenty minutes, I'm turning figure eights on the on- and off-ramps of Charlotte proper, trying to find my way north. For a while I think that we might never actually make it out of the winding web of the city, but eventually we do. I find the exit and follow Highway 74 up out of the confusing city traffic as it climbs through the Great Smoky Mountains.

Through the dirty, bug-specked windshield of our mile-worn minivan, I keep trying to take pictures. But there is no way to capture the magnitude of the landscape around us.

The road curves in and out and around, and semis drive past breathlessly close, and we're *thisclose* to dropping off the side of the world.

This is where the Cherokee Indians told stories to their children about a magical lake hidden somewhere within the range, inaccessible to humans. This is where the mountains became a kind of dividing line between the Union North and Confederate South, where neighbor was separated from neighbor by the towering of rock and belief and pride.

This is where loggers felled trees and sent them down the rivers to lumber mills. This is where Dolly Parton was born and raised, strumming country songs about the Smoky Mountain fir trees on her first guitar.

It's where my mother spent a college summer—working at an ice-cream shop in the touristy town of Gatlinburg with Campus Crusade for Christ, trying to spread the Gospel. This is where I spent a day once, too—on yet another Lightrider trip—hiking into the mountains. I'd tied my long-sleeved shirt around my waist and hoisted myself up, grasping for the next handhold on steep paths. I was seventeen, no stranger by then to heartbreak or to my own weakness. But as I breathed the mountain air during that long Smoky Mountain hike, I learned that I could do it. That I was strong. That I was *brave*.

We're supposed to have dinner and spend the night with friends in Louisville, but by lunchtime I already know we're not going to make it. At a McDonald's somewhere in the middle of the Smoky Mountains, I look at the map again and again, recalculating the miles. There's no way around it: There are too many hours still to drive. Too much ground to cover. We won't hit Louisville until after nine o'clock, and by then the kids will be passed out in the back. I send an apologetic text message and cancel.

I pick at my fries while Liam blasts through the tube slide and falls onto the rubber floor mat, laughing. He shoots up and yells "Minja Turtle power!" and his face is glowing red as he turns around and hoofs it back up the play structure. *I'm ready to be home.*

"I have good news," I tell Andrew when he picks up the phone.

"What's that?"

"We have officially collected not one but *two* sets of all the McDonald's *Lego Movie* cups."

"What?"

"It's what they're giving away with Happy Meals right now. Reusable, holographic, *Lego Movie* theme cups. We have them all. Twice."

"Sweet."

"I know, right?" I say, eating another one of the kids' abandoned french fries off the tray. "Score!"

He laughs. "So where are you guys?"

"McDonald's-ing somewhere in the Smoky Mountains."

"Cool."

"Yeah. I decided that I'm going to skip my Louisville stop and just drive into the night."

"Wow. You sure?"

"Yeah. I think I should be able to get to my parents' house by around one. Two at the latest." Dane is following Liam up the tiered platforms of the play area, giving him boosts when he can't wiggle up to the next step. "Look, Mom!" he shouts. "I'm helpin' Liam!" I give him the biggest smile I can and a hearty thumbs-up, and he beams back at me from behind the black netting. "I think we're all just ready to be home."

"Well, Marty and I are definitely ready to have you home."

"How's the weather? Nice and warm?"

"Definitely," he lies. "Should be . . . let's see . . . negative nine on Friday when you get home."

"Mmm. *Balmy*," I say.

We talk a while longer. He's had his first interview now, for a possible new job, and the manager has already called back for a second. "Go, Presh!" I say, and he laughs.

I tell him about the kids and about Rob and Debbie, about the horse and the collection of moss that Dane garnered this morning during a brisk walk on their property. He tells me about work, about the guys he's been hanging out with, about how quiet the house is without us. He reminds me to drive safe, and I promise that I will. "I love you," he says. "I miss you."

"I love you, too."

As I hang up, I think about him at home, padding up to the kitchen in his blue jeans and wool socks to make himself lunch in our empty house. Eleven years of marriage, in love, too, has turned out to be much less about the electric current of passion than about these five-minute phone calls, about making dinner, chopping peppers, stirring the risotto on the stove. About night-time Netflix marathons, about standing at the thresholds of our children's rooms at night, watching them sleep.

It had turned out to be about becoming comfortable with each other's silences—about the paradoxical way that pulling back and giving each other pockets of space draws us closer.

In high school, when I was busy *acquiring the fire,* I thought that those life-defining things like *faith* and *love* had to be all passion and emotion to be real. The faith story I was learning to tell took its cue from mass-produced page-turners—sticky trade paperbacks, Harlequin love stories, fluffy and forgettable and action-packed. It was all plot and climax, bodice-ripping and James Bond—and not really true.

The life that Andrew and I are living now, at the very beginning of the middle of our lives, has turned out to have little in the way of plot-forwarding excitement. Little in the way of *life-and-death* drama. And I'd created more trouble than story by seeking out that tension in car windows and bars. In an attempt to *feel it more,* I hadn't made my life more interesting. Just more shattered.

Now I gather up the shoes from the sweat-slick red cubbies and dump our lunch remains from the tray into the garbage. "Come on, you Ninja Turtles!" I shout up into the tubes. "Time to hit the road." While I wait for them, tapping my toes on the sticky surface of the linoleum floor, it occurs to me that maybe faith was never meant to be some perfectly plotted, passion-driven paperback. Maybe faith is the long story of a happy marriage—an average life made fuller, not smaller, by the pockets of silence and darkness that break into it.

The people of Kentucky are doing their Wednesday-night grocery run at Walmart. They are buying milk and cheese, boxes of macaroni, gym socks and laundry detergent and new tubes of Crest toothpaste and tampons. Their carts are filled with the basics, stacked high with the stuff of everyday living. Mountains of toilet paper, towering twenty-four-packs of bottled water, economy-size bags of off-brand breakfast cereal.

My cart is empty, except for Liam, who is standing inside it, not holding on. "You're going to fall," I tell him. "You're gonna get an owie. You need to sit down." He just grins impishly at me, a close-lipped smile that goes right to the corners of his eyes. I shake my head.

We're at this Kentucky interstate Walmart because it's dinnertime, and I couldn't fathom another McDonald's, another cardboard box of french fries, the smell of oil hanging in the air, the spinny-chaired table that Liam and Dane would inevitably choose. I have reached my McLimit.

So . . . Walmart. It's no quirky small-town diner with a blue-plate special, but at least here I can find something different to eat. A deli sandwich, maybe. Some kind of vegetable, perhaps.

When we got out of the car in the Walmart parking lot ten minutes ago, we were all slapped by a freezing gust of northern air. "Cold!" Dane screamed, pulling his sweatshirt hood up. "Cold, cold, cold!"

"Hold you!" Liam said, and I picked him up, pulled his hood over his ears. *When did this happen?* I thought as I grabbed Dane's hand. Without realizing it, I'd driven through some invisible line crossing the country, bisecting it into Warm and Not-Warm, and we're officially in the Not-Warm part again. "Run! Let's just run fast!" I said, and we did—sprinted through the automatic Walmart doors, past the blue-vested elderly greeter, and into the warmth.

Now I wander the aisles aimlessly, Liam inside the cart, Dane walking next to it. I do it not really because we need anything but just to move, just to not be in the car. I walk us through the clearance aisle with its assortment of red-stickered merchandise. Past Rubbermaid and towels and flimsy full-length mirrors and laundry baskets. It's oddly comforting to me, to be in this big-box kind of normalcy. We could be anywhere. We could even be home.

From the toy aisle, I let each of the boys pick out a small toy, knowing as he chooses it that Dane will regret the tiny clearance Skylanders play-set he's holding. I buy a *Lego Ninjago* DVD for the car, hoping that what I'm actually paying for with that ten dollars is an hour or two of quiet.

In the grocery section of the store, rows of neatly stacked packaged foods make me instantly hungry. Into the cart go two prepared turkey wraps, a pack of Juicy Juice boxes, and a dark chocolate Milky Way bar. Dane keeps trying to show random people his new toy. When they respond to him, he glows with pride. When they don't, he falls flat-faced onto the white tile Walmart floor, sobbing between Rollback pallets of Gatorade and ramen noodles.

Outside, I assemble peanut-butter sandwiches while standing in the shocking winter cold of the Kentucky parking lot. The loaf of bread that I've had with me since Nashville is a little bit flattened and almost expired, but I use it anyway, lathering it haphazardly with Jif and slapping it together. I open juice boxes and punch plastic straws through foil-covered holes. I unwrap the new toys and the new movie. While I'm trying to get the DVD to play, Dane drops a couple of the pieces of his play-set into the dark, crumb-filled crevices of the van and begins to wail, so I get on my hands and knees under the dome light and feel around until I find them.

The movie starts. I crank the heat and take my contacts out, throw my hair on top of my head, and put on my glasses. I'm gearing up for the long haul—a late night of driving alone. I want to be comfortable. On the way out of the Walmart parking lot, I detour into a McDonald's drive-through, where I buy a large Diet Coke. The cup it comes in is awkward and Styrofoam, and I lodge it into the van's cup holder while I steer out of this anonymous Kentucky town and get back on the highway.

As we merge onto the mountain road, I steel myself for the next several hours of lonely night driving. The mountains around me are shadowed and stoic, and I try to summon that thing I felt at seventeen when I was pulling myself up into them: strength, bravery—that deep well of confidence that *I could do this*.

I pull at the cup of Diet Coke, but it's a bit too big for the cup holder, and it's wedged. I pull a little harder. Then a little harder than that. As I do, my thumb punches through the Styrofoam. *Crack*. The cup crumbles beneath my hand in one sickening instant.

On the narrow two-lane road, semis are thundering toward us, weaving around us, making the car shake with their sheer proximity. There's nowhere to pull over—at least nowhere that I can see in the falling evening dark. Diet Coke is gushing onto my lap, soaking my quarter-eaten deli wrap, and I'm trying to throw that doomed, borrowed phone and iPod and wallet out of the way while also staying on the road, swearing under my breath as the pop drips down my legs and into my boots.

Dane starts crying. "I don't *like* this show, Mom!" he screams from the back. The next exit is five miles down the road. I'm so thirsty that I try to take a drink of the Diet Coke from the cracked-open side of the cup. Predictably, this makes things even worse.

"I'M TALKIN' TO YOU, MOM!" Dane roars.

"I HEARD YOU!" I scream back.

The next five miles feel infinite. The Diet Coke is seeping through my jeans, and Dane is screaming behind me. Because he hates the movie—*"I don't want this! I don't! I don't!"*—Liam screaming because he can't *hear* the movie—*"Stop, Dane!"*

The headlights are careening toward us on the two-lane mountain road and then disappearing into the dark. When we finally make it to the exit, I pull into the first empty parking spot of the first gas station I see, waddle out of the driver's seat in my soaked-through clothes, slam the door, and jerk the trunk open to look for a fresh outfit and a dry beach towel.

"What are you doing, Mom!" Dane demands to know.

"COLD!" Liam whines.

"I know," I say, rifling through the totes. Such a stupid idea, these totes. I can't find a damn thing.

"WHAT ARE YOU DOING, MOM!" Dane repeats, louder still.

"I spilled. I need to change my clothes."

"What did you say?"

"COLD!" Liam repeats.

"Mom! WHAT DID YOU SAY?"

"COLD! COLD! COLD!!!"

I change clothes in the driver's seat, twisting between the steering wheel and the seat back, trying to strip wet clothes off in the strained fluorescent light of the gas-station windows, hoping that no one in the clogged, rush-hour traffic next to us is looking this way. Dane has lots of questions about what spilled, where it spilled, what's happening, and also, *WHY ARE WE STILL WATCHING*

THIS SHOW? I mop up the Diet Coke as best I can and sit down on the beach towel. The whole thing feels like a passive-aggressive welcome back to the North. *Nice,* I mumble—to God, to the icy northern world, to no one in particular. *Very nice.*

"CHANGE THE MOVIE!" Dane screams as I start the car, finally ready to go. I smack my head against the steering wheel until I accidentally make it honk. Then I get out of the car and walk, simmering, to Dane's side to change the movie.

"How's that?" I say through gritted teeth, and he must sense that I'm on the brink of total meltdown, because he says, "Good." And then adds a quick "Thanks . . . my beautiful mother."

We drive on.

Behind me the light from the movie flickers across Dane's and Liam's face as they drift off to sleep, their heads drooping to the side, necks bent heavily toward their respective windows. I exhale, flip off the DVD player, and turn on my audiobook, cautiously, checking in the rearview mirror for stirrings from the boys. I'm on the last disc of *Loving Frank,* and I'm ready to finish.

Things seem to be turning around for Mamah, just a bit. She's managed to make peace with her two children—the ones from whom she's been estranged ever since she abandoned them for Frank all those years ago. She's planting a garden at Taliesin. All seems to be right with the world.

Except then Joyce's voice turns a little dark, a little foreboding, as she begins to describe the odd, passive-aggressive actions of a household butler named Julian. "Cut him loose, Mamah," I tell the book. But she doesn't, and it's not much longer before the manic-faced butler sets aflame the terrace on which Mamah and her kids are eating lunch and then blocks the exit holding an ax.

"What?! Don't say it, Joyce," I beg. "This is *not* how this book ends."

But Joyce *does* say it. She describes the death of Mamah, sparing no grisly detail—not even the sounds of her children as they are hacked to death trying to flee the burning terrace. I drive several moments in a state of horrified shock until the book ends and Joyce's voice evaporates into the darkness, leaving me all alone in the minivan.

I take the disc out of the CD player and fling it onto the pile of crap on the passenger seat. I feel shaken and unsettled and a little lost in space and time. "Gah," I say out loud to no one in particular, shaking my head back and forth, as if the movement might clear away the inky remains of the story, staining my imagination. *There go thirteen hours and thirty-eight minutes of my life,* I think. *I should have gone with Jane Austen. No one ever gets hacked to death in a Jane Austen book.*

Liam stirs and lets out a whimper. "Shhh," I say. "You're okay." I fumble with my iPod until I find the kids' lullaby playlist—the one with the covers of hymns that we've been listening to every night.

"Mama," he says.

"I'm here." I reach back and rub his bare foot. I've gotten used to this awkward turn of the body. This reaching back toward him while still driving us forward.

From the iHome on the dashboard, an intimate rendition of "The Lord's Prayer" floats through the van, and I feel myself relax a little into the still-damp driver's seat. The mountains disappear behind us, and we are caught in the dark thrumming of a Kentucky plainsong, driving.

> *Father in heaven*
> *Hallowed be thy name.*
> *Your kingdom come, your will be done*
> *Here as in heaven.*

Liam's eyes flutter closed, and he rests his head against the padded side of his car seat. The waning moon is a thumbnail, a perfect crescent—12 percent visible but still casting so much light on the ice-painted fields. I carefully let go of Liam's foot and crane my neck toward the windshield to look up. Sure enough: *stars.*

There are a hundred thousand of them, flung wildly across the clear, cold sky. Beyond them three hundred billion more that I cannot see, and beyond *them* the sun—lighting the other side of the world right now, making herself known only as she is reflected in the dark heart of the moon.

How do you know God is real?

It's like this: Once upon a time, I learned that God came like light. I spent a long time, head against the window, peering into the darkness, praying for God to come like a spotlight, like a fire, like some wild laser show in the pitch-black sky. I learned to fear the darkness, and when it came, I struck myself against everything around me, trying to make sparks.

How do you know God is real?

I think about the faith journey described in the Bible, and it occurs to me that while there are miracles—moments when God appears and you feel him absolutely—they're mostly few and far between. This is not a string of heart-pounding moments, a television episode, an Acquire the Fire conference. Really, it's much quieter. Softer. Longer. Boring, even. Faith spans years, generations, millennia. It's built into the calendar, the day, the seasons, and it's possible that you could forget to notice it.

Morning. Evening.

Light. Dark.

High tide. Low tide.

Every now and then, God appears to his people in the blazing fire, flaming and luminous and breathtaking. But it's less often than I always thought. And his silence marks the pages of the biblical narrative more than I ever knew. In fact, God has a history of going quiet with his people.

His silence stretches over years, over countries, over generations. But it's not an abandonment, it's an invitation. It asks something different of us than the fire does. It asks for our trust, for our hope, for us to *stay* as the night darkens around us and we can't hear a thing.

In the middle of rural Kentucky, I still don't really feel God. Not as I once did. I feel the damp beach towel beneath me and the subtle shaking of the van and the wind sweeping across the plains, pushing against my vehicle ever so slightly. That's it. There is no voice from heaven breaking the silence, no sudden angel choir bursting through, no shooting star flung suddenly across the sky. This is not a movie montage; there is no climax to this story. Instead the same darkness that has been following me all this time presses in on us. Again.

This time I let it.

Overhead, the stars shine. I feel myself grow small and disappear into the dark wonder of it—and I am not afraid. *I am not afraid.* The dark sky hems me in, and I hold my breath.

> *Give us this day*
> *Our daily bread*
> *Forgive us our debts*
> *As we forgive . . .*

All my life, I think, I've misunderstood. Jesus is the Light of the world, the Scripture says. I sang it with my arms raised. I told it to my uncomprehending classmates and tattooed it on my binder with puffy paint. I believed that I understood what it meant, so I drove to Lake Michigan in the earliest parts of the morning to feel it.

I hadn't understood, then, that love doesn't always look like romance and faith doesn't look like fire and light doesn't always look like the sun—and that this *matters.*

Jesus is the Light of the world. In him there is no darkness, the Bible says. But there are so many different ways that Light manifests itself. It's the pinks and oranges of a summer dawn. It's the full, bright sun glancing off the wave tips of the ocean. The hazy winter starlight. The shivering, waning moon. The falling dusk, still glowing like a promise at the edges of the world.

> *And lead us not into temptation,*
> *Deliver us from evil.*

I don't feel God now any more than I did at the beginning of this trip. But I understand all at once that this is beside the point.

God is as close as the air around us, as true as the North Star leading me home. In the dark Kentucky plain, my eyes adjust, and there is so much that I can't see—and also so much that I *can*. Mostly that the darkness was never really *dark*. And that it was never my job to turn on the lights.

> *For thine is the kingdom and the power and the glory*
> *For thine is the kingdom and the power and the glory*

Out here on the highway, the slivered moon is shining and the stars are bright, and I can't see much. But what I *can* see is beautiful.

Glory, the voice on the album sings. *Glory. Glory.*

I shift on the beach towel and feel the Diet Coke damp on my jeans. The passenger seat of the van is piled high with the scattered remains of our road-trip supplies. Wrappers and orphaned CDs and the broken pieces of my Styrofoam cup, still dripping with caramel color. The thin moon cuts through the clouds and streams through the window, baptizing the whole messy thing in a pool of light. *Glory,* I sing softly with the album. Then, louder, on the brink of tears. *Glory. Glory.* And in the dark Kentucky night, I know that God is real. And it's not because I feel him. It's because the night is dark and bright all at once, because the stars are an infinite repeating liturgy lighting the way back home. I know because *I know*. It's as simple and mysterious as that.

Glory.

Chicago, Illinois, to Andover, Minnesota (aka . . . Home)

Thursday, February 27, to Friday, February 28, 2014

By the time I wake up the next morning, the lazy February sunshine has already made its way into the sky and is dousing me in watery winter light. I rub at my eyes, which feel crusted over and itchy, and when I finally pry them open, I find myself all alone in my little brother's old bedroom. On the wall above me, there is a framed picture of him in a pool, his spiky fifth-grade buzz glistening with water.

It takes me a minute to piece it all together—where I am, how we got here—but then it all comes back. Thirteen hours of driving in one day, the snow-covered Indiana plains, the field of white windmills glowing in the dark. The Chicago traffic arching around the city under the watching eyes of the billboards. Pulling into my parents' driveway at last. What time was that? Two, maybe? Three? I can't remember. All I remember is the numbing windchill cutting into my face as I lifted my boys from their car seats and hauled them, half asleep, into the house.

Through the thin walls of my parents' suburban rambler, I can hear spoons clanking and my mom's upbeat voice in the kitchen, followed immediately by Dane's—loud and uninhibited, wild with excitement. Then a raspy squeak that could only belong to Liam. I smile into the blankets. This is the first morning in two weeks that I've woken up by myself. It feels delicious.

When I finally make my way out of the bedroom and trundle into the living room, bleary-eyed in my sweatpants, every toy is spread out on the floor and abandoned, and Grandma, Dane, and Liam are in the kitchen. The boys are standing on chairs that have been pulled up next to the counter. "We're making a cake for Papi!" Dane says, holding up a spatula dripping with chocolate batter.

"Cool," I croak, looking for a coffee mug.

"Hi, sweetie!" Mom says. She gives me a hearty kiss on the cheek and then holds my shoulders, looks at my face, and smiles. "Did you sleep well?"

"*So* well," I say, walking a few steps to the coffeemaker. I survey the half pot of coffee inside. My dad is in the habit of brewing one pot at the beginning of the week and then reheating it day after day until it's gone. "How long has this been here?" I ask tentatively.

She smiles. "I made you a new pot this morning."

"You love me."

"I do," she says, and I can hear the grin in her voice as she bends over the counter to help Dane crack eggs gently against the bowl. "Like this," she says to him. "Yes! Great job!" Then to me she adds, "We decided to celebrate Papi's birthday early."

"I see that."

"Yeah! And we're going to get him presents!" Dane says, waving the spatula around, flicking bits of batter onto the cabinets and floor. I grimace, but Mom doesn't seem to notice.

"So," she says, "tell me about the trip."

I sigh and sit down at the kitchen table. Where to start? How to sum up an Epic Winter Road Trip? How to explain what it was like, driving 3,501.2 miles—give or take—alone with my kids? Alone with myself. How to talk about the adventure of it, the grind of it? I think about the rain washing the snow away for the first time as we drove out of Indiana. I think about that sinkhole in Bowling Green, about the dead fish and the live ones, gas stations and guest rooms and semis. I think about the driver's seat and the passenger seat and the greasy chip bags and the used napkins and the empty sippy cups rolling round.

I think about my own heart—a shell at low tide, emptied out and waiting to be swept up again. I think about Sarah touching the rounding orb of her pregnant belly and Leigh handing me a mug brownie. About Jake with his careful kindness and Matt and Audrey—their old iPhone pressed into my hands when I needed it most. Julie and Josh. Rob and Debbie. All those people, welcoming us as we made our way away from—then back toward—home.

"The trip." I sigh. I take a long drink of coffee and shake my head. "It was really something."

All morning the kids and Grandma bake boxed cake, tape streamers to the wall, and blow up balloons. In the afternoon Liam fights with me about taking a nap, but in the end he passes out next to me in the double bed of Erik's old room, arm flung over his head, breathing steadily. Dane and Grandma leave to buy presents for Papi at the Dollar Store, and I lie in bed next to Liam, breathing in the sweet smell of his skin, pressing my lips against his hair.

We don't leave for Minnesota until well after dinner. I wait until the kids have eaten and sung "Happy Birthday" and given my dad his carefully wrapped gifts—"Army men! How did you know I wanted these?" I wait until the first yawns begin rising from their tiny bodies—and that's when I finally load the van one last time, buckle them into their car seats, and say good-bye.

I'll drive late into the night, just as I did yesterday. Just as I've done so many times before. I'd forgotten the solace of this—night driving, the boys sleeping behind me, the moon glowing ahead. I have a travel mug of freshly brewed coffee and a new audiobook. It's only 409 miles from here to home—six hours and sixteen minutes. *I've got this.*

"Last trip!" I tell the boys as I pull the van slowly out of the driveway and honk softly at my parents, who are standing in the threshold of the house, waving. "Last long car ride. When you wake up, we'll be home."

"Home?" Liam asks, wide-eyed.

"YES!" Dane says, pumping the air with his fist. "And I get to see my toys and my bed and my room and . . . oh! My door, Mom! My door!"

"I know." I smile at him in the rearview mirror.

I drive slowly out of my parents' neighborhood and onto the main drag of my youth. To the left I see my old high school with its snow-covered sports fields and its giant, circular EXCELLENCE IN EDUCATION seal. The orange text on its computerized marquee is scrolling through upcoming school events. BLOOD DRIVE. EXPRESSIONS SHOW CHOIR CONCERT. PARENT-TEACHER CONFERENCES. Echoes from another lifetime.

The flagpole is still in the middle of the circular driveway, flanked by the brown brick walls of the school, and I can barely remember what it felt like to stand there every year on national See You at the Pole Day to pray aloud. I can hardly remember what it felt like to be fifteen, filled with such exuberant, fiery faith. *I'm a Christian. But not, you know, a* weird *Christian.* What had it felt like, *really*, to get on a train downtown to Chicago, to stand and sing loud to Jesus without a hint of cynicism or doubt? To *acquire the fire* and hold it in my bones? I can't remember, no matter how hard I try.

The light turns red, and I sit there looking at the flagpole, thinking of that old version of me. There she stood—small and sure, not a twanging gray hair in sight—praying in the open, feeling the righteous glow of it, the passion, the purity. *I can almost see her.* And for the first time in a long time, I don't feel pity or frustration or cynicism or nostalgia when I do. Instead I think about landscape and seasons. About how it's not really all that odd that she felt so *on fire,* so bright during those years. She was at the summer start of her journey of faith. She was waiting at the beach with the seagulls. She was getting her first glimpse of God.

The light changes, and I drive slowly away from the school, through the suburban landscape of my former life. There is the Panera where I used to meet Kim and Alissa after school to talk about Jesus. There is the restaurant parking lot where we used to park our cars during school before they started towing. That fitness club used to be a movie theater. That IHOP used to be a fancy French restaurant.

It was, of course, a lifetime ago: we all used to be different. The seasons turn, and we turn with them—and if we're very lucky—or very careful—we're constantly turning into truer versions of ourselves.

By the time we soar through the first electronic toll on I-94 West, the kids are asleep. They were so tired when we left that I didn't even bother turning on the movie. "Look at the trees," I suggested, and they did. They sat there, staring up out of the windows as we merged onto the last of the long highways. Past the Belvedere Oasis, around Rockford, out of Illinois and into Wisconsin. *Loves Park. Roscoe. Rockton. Beloit.*

I know the outskirts of each of these towns. Over the last several years, I have become intimately acquainted with the generic places where they intersect with the highway. Shell stations and SuperAmericas and Mobils. Arby's and Burger King and, of course, McDonald's. Commonplace stops. Not glamorous, but full, still, of generosity and kindness, brokenness and beauty. It's bored teenage clerks, half stoned behind the counter. It's single mothers working long hours at this highway stop, missing their kids and still mustering the grace to smile at mine.

If I'd thought about faith as a *journey* in my life, I'd never pictured anything as average as all that. I'd imagined the same spontaneous and whimsical road trip I thought I'd be taking these past couple of weeks. I'd envisioned back roads, detours, oddities, quirky characters, and brilliant insights. In my faith fiction, I'd pictured myself growing wiser with each golden day, sitting at the sun-dappled kitchen table, looking adoringly at a glowing white Jesus. In this fantasy I'd been gypsy-free in the grace of it all—living a summertime road-trip faith, staring at the Light through my sunglasses, shaking loose my curls, taking my kids by the hand, leading them gently around every roadblock toward a God they would always be able to see.

As it turns out, this version of my faith journey is every bit as fictional as the road trip I'd imagined.

In the quiet dark of Interstate 94, I sip my coffee and think about all the miles behind us, the miles before us—every last one stretched longer than I thought possible by Kid Time. I'm at the helm of the minivan, surrounded by string-cheese wrappers and sippy cups, nondescript on the asphalt surface of the earth. Just another minivan, just another mom, hair in a ponytail, glasses on, sweatshirt ragged around the ends of the sleeves.

This is no one's road-trip fantasy—least of all mine.

And yet.

The scrappy moon peers out from somewhere north of here. Five percent visible—nearly as small as it will get before it seems to disappear entirely. For a day or two, the new moon will look like a phantom shadow, but then, slowly, it will begin to grow again. *Waxing crescent. Waxing gibbous. Full moon.*

Maybe faith has never been anything more than this slow, steady process of change. Foot on the gas pedal, moving forward through the nondescript dark. Waxing and waning in an ever-present Light.

In the book of Mark, there is an orphaned verse that describes Jesus' "quiet time" routine. *Very early in the morning, while it was still dark, Jesus got up, left the house, and went off to a solitary place, where he prayed.*

I always took this verse as a sort of instruction—a simple how-to for a vibrant life of faith. *Get up early. Have a "quiet time." Carve out moments to meet with God alone at the beginning of the day.* Certainly that was how it was always presented to me in my spiritually ambitious youth, surrounded as I was with so many Christians who glowed happily.

The verse comes just after another about the miracles that Jesus has performed, the things he has done, the demons he has cast out and away. *See?* the fired-up spiritual teachers said from the front of large auditoriums, and we trembled before them like a thousand tiny flames, listening, nodding. *You want to do great things for God? Then you have to make time to be* alone *with him.* And we'd all recommitted our lives to quiet mornings with Jesus.

But maybe that's only part of the point. Maybe there's something else there: Jesus, stumbling out into the darkness. *There he is,* under the thin light of the stars. Like Moses, he is moving resolutely toward the thick darkness of God, of the world itself. The verse doesn't tell us much more, but I have to assume that it's not the end of the story—just the beginning. That he went into the darkness, and he found something amazing, something beautiful, something worthy of all his wonder.

In the Exodus narrative, it's not long after the series of plagues—one of them being the all-consuming darkness *that can be felt*—that the people of Israel are freed from Egypt, only to find themselves lost in the open wound of wilderness. It's in this tenuous, trying space that they will spend so many years learning to follow God. But they don't know that yet.

What they *do* know is that from the heart of a dense smoke and the trembling top of Mount Sinai, God is speaking over them, calling them his treasured possession, calling them holy, giving them a new law. And then, as the people remain at a distance, *Moses approached the thick darkness where God was*. He stays there, in the darkness of God, for forty days and forty nights, Scripture tells us. When he comes down, they say, his face is radiant.

The tree line breaks again, and I can see Cascade Mountain rising on the south side of the road, the snow lit by a dozen lights, the silhouettes of skiers and snowboarders cutting down the slopes. Just beyond this are the Dells, the Pizza Pub closing up for the night, the off-season hotels blinking Vacancy signs in the emptied-out Thursday-night Wisconsin cold. Beyond that, Tomah, with its eight thousand fast-food restaurants and towering highway Walmart, then Menomonie, fraught with cop cars sitting in turnabouts, lights off, waiting.

I tick the cities off in my head: Eau Claire, Hudson, and then we're almost there. The bridge will arc over the icy Mississippi River, the moon glistening off her inky waters, and then we'll be there, the big WELCOME TO MINNESOTA sign waving us home.

SCENARIO: You are driving seventy-eight miles an hour on the long, flat highway, the glinting dark road ahead of you like the surface of the moon. You're thinking of home and of your husband. Of the road behind you and the one before you. Thinking of the quirky girl in that road-trip movie *Elizabethtown,* handing the main character a map through his pain. "Begin your journey. Do not skip ahead," she says.

Outside the windows the waning crescent moon is creating haunting silhouettes of the bare branches in the night, framing the whole thing in silver, drawing us forward.

I couldn't skip ahead if I wanted to. And for the first time in two weeks, two years, two decades, maybe, I don't.

A sign flashes by. MINNEAPOLIS—240 MILES.

I press my foot to the gas pedal and watch the speedometer creep up: *74, 76, 78.* I can get home by one in the morning if I don't make any stops.

EPILOGUE

November 2014—
Nine Months Later

It's getting cold again in Minnesota. The pond in our back-yard is beginning to freeze over, and just last week we turned back the clocks an hour. *Welcome to the Dark Season,* I say to myself as the last strands of light fade out of the sky while I'm making dinner at night. *Do not be afraid.*

Right now there are a hundred mallard ducks in the backyard. Our next-door neighbor, Bill, raised a few abandoned ones from ducklings in his garage a few years ago, and even though they're gone now, he still brings out big paint buckets filled with corn every evening and scatters it across the grass for the others.

At sunset the ducks waddle up from the pond and eat their fill. Dane and Liam have gotten into the habit of chasing them, running at full sprint across the yard until the ducks get tired of running and rise up in a cloud of feathers and squawks and land back on the pond. A few minutes later, they'll try again—single file, marching up the grassy banks of suburban backyards toward the food. The whole thing could continue for hours if I don't call the boys in for dinner.

I know how this goes. I've seen it happen every year. The ducks will stay as long as they can. The pond will continue to freeze, and the open space of water will get smaller and smaller. The ducks will persist in their flapping toward the center, trying like mad to keep it unfrozen by the sheer force of their collective will. But one of these nights, the ice will creep in too far and the ducks will surrender. All at once they'll lift off the pond, and for one suspended moment they'll hover over the ice. Then they'll go.

They'll sweep up over the top of our house, over our quiet neighborhood street and over Hanson Boulevard, over Andover itself, a wide, wild V against the orange sunset. They will follow the map of their bodies. They will follow the light, guided by the stars, pulled by the earth itself. *South.*

If I'm lucky enough to see their departure, I'll stand there for a long time, watching. Wishing I could follow. Feeling, too, the siren southern song, thinking of the beach and the sand, thinking of the light streaming over the water.

Then I'll turn around and go inside.

Dane is in kindergarten now. He's five years old, outgrowing his blue jeans every other month, getting tall. His face has thinned out, lost every last trace of baby fat, and his arms are strong and lanky. He's learning to read and write simple words. *And. The. It. Mom. Dad.*

Car.

Go.

Sun. Moon.

Stay.

Every morning Dane pulls on his coat and gloves and hat. He straps on his backpack and stands by the front door. "*Mom!* Come on! It's time to go to the bus!" Liam sits crisscross-applesauce on the living-room carpet in his pajamas, zoned in to *Curious George*, pressing tiny Legos into one another.

"Want to come to the bus stop with us?" I ask him as I pull my own boots and hat on over my sweatpants and bedhead. Mostly he says, "No. I stay here."

Liam is three, speaking more and more in full sentences now, starting to dress himself, becoming more independent every single day. "Okay," I tell him. "Be right back." And then Dane and I run outside, follow along the curb of our sidewalkless street next door to Bill's driveway. We huddle together with our hands in our coat pockets and wait for the halting yellow bus to screech to a stop at the corner.

This morning the first winter winds have been blowing sharply against us as we stand there waiting, and Dane's cheeks turn bright red. "I don't want to go outside at recess today Mom," he says with a sigh, leaning against me. "It's *cold*." His voice is bordering on hysterical whining.

"Listen," I say, crouching down in Bill's driveway to zip his coat to the top and pull his hat down more snugly over his ears. "You are strong and brave. It will feel really cold at first, but if you run and play, soon you'll hardly even notice it."

He nods skeptically.

"Hug?"

Dane loops his arms around me and kisses me smack on the mouth as the bus rolls up next to us. I don't know how many years I have left of these shameless, extravagant displays of affection, and I feel the weight of gratitude as he pulls away and runs toward the bus.

I watch my son climb up the steps and say hello to Fred, the elderly bus driver with the full gray beard. Dane waves and blows kisses out the first-row window, and I wave and kiss back, until the bus disappears around the corner.

The wind cuts across the expanse of the driveway, and I shiver. Sigh.

It's possible. I could pull him out of school if I really wanted to. We could leave again, drive to Florida and back. I've done it before, and I could do it again. I'd do it better this time. Plan it more carefully. I'd carve out time to see the caves in Kentucky. I'd spend more time in Nashville. We'd do Atlanta instead of Covington, and on the way home we'd take the gondola up the Smoky Mountains in Gatlinburg. We'd stand at the top of the mountain and point at the sloping wonder and feel strong.

I'd take a different route. I'd skip the tote bags, maybe, book more hotels, go to SeaWorld.

It's tempting. The first cuts of winter are slicing into my skin, and it would be so nice to *go,* to shake the winter off my boots and leave.

Perhaps the drive to escape will always be inside me. Maybe I'll always feel nostalgic for the idea of *warmth,* of endless summer, of the shards of sunlight sitting at the tips of ocean waters.

But also—this is his home. Our home. *My home.* This is the place I have chosen and that has chosen me. And so this year our Epic Winter Road Trip will loop along the roads of this familiar Minneapolis suburb, through the landscape that we find ourselves in. *We are strong and brave,* I think as I walk briskly home from the bus stop—cold but *okay* in my winter boots, my wool mittens, my striped gray hat. *We were built to stay.*

It's nighttime again. The dishes are done, and the kids are in bed after Andrew has settled under our green duvet cover with his book. I come downstairs to prep the coffee and get a glass of water and take my pill. The pill is no bigger than the smallest of ocean pebbles. I take it every single night before I go to sleep.

For a long time, I thought the antidepressant's purpose was to dispel the darkness. But now I understand that the darkness was never really the enemy—not in the way I once thought it was. The pill I take is about realigning the neurotransmitters in my brain—but I think that's just a fancy way of saying that it's about helping my eyes remember how to adjust to the darkness. It's about helping me to see.

After all, there is so much here: My sons growing tall and independent and beautiful. My husband with his generous smile, his deep crow's-feet, his familiar laugh. The dog, stretched out on the couch, snoring softly into the throw blanket. The neighbors, silhouettes against their windows, living their own routine, beautiful lives.

I wander out onto the deck in my hooded sweatshirt and yoga pants. The moon is thin, and the stars are as bright as they can be in the suburbs. I lie down on the wooden slats of the deck and look up. I can see my breath in the air for the first time this year, forming soft silver puffs above my head. In the sky the light of God reflects off the dark surface of the moon and makes shadowed paths on the half-frozen grass in our backyard.

At the bottom of our pond, the painted turtles are busy tunneling deep into the sand and mud, slowing their breath, settling. The dormouse is burrowing herself into some hidden hollow, letting her temperature drop to nearly freezing, trusting that she will wake again when the time is right.

The leaves on the oaks and maples and ash trees lit themselves orange and red and yellow last month, and it was beautiful. But so is what's happening now in the silent stillness of their empty branches: the dead cells freezing solid while the living ones next to them somehow remain unfrozen. It is a purposeful, mysterious kind of dormancy. It's possible, of course, to prevent a tree from wintering if you keep it inside with a stable temperature and light pattern. But I read somewhere that if it's never allowed to go dormant, if it's forced to endure an "eternal summer," the tree will die every single time.

Somewhere, far away from here, ducks are beginning to migrate, following the map of the stars. Our posse of stubborn mallards is quacking softly on the pond, but I know they'll be leaving soon, too. Anyway, I'm not thinking about them just now. I'm thinking about the trees and the turtles. I'm thinking about the dormouse, her heart beating only once every few minutes, sustained somehow by stillness.

I breathe in, breathe out, feel the cold, sharp air in my lungs. It's almost winter. This time I'm going to let it be winter.

I don't have any rituals, rites, escapes, or solutions this time around, except to let my heart become very still. I will drive Liam to preschool and go to church and do the dishes. I will get up in the mornings and open my Bible, and if I feel nothing, I'll stay still anyway.

It's not up to me to flip on the lights. The Light is already here.

I will continue to navigate my tricky relationship with my emotions. Sometimes I'll drink too much wine and wake up hungover and regretful. Sometimes I'll binge-watch TV until I feel closer to character constructs than I do to God. A man will flirt in some Target line some average Monday when I'm feeling weak, and for a second I'll forget that it's not real and I'll let it in.

I'll fail, fall, flatten out—and that's all part of it. The rhythm, the seasons—a faith that looks less like a steady climb toward glory and more like a tangled, curling road map that nonetheless is headed somewhere good.

And some nights I hope I will have the courage to leave the shows off altogether and put down the glass of wine and instead come out here, on this deck. I can imagine myself here, standing for a while in the cold, prickling stillness, uncomfortable and half frozen and wanting to go in.

But then—*the light*. The ombré of the night sky, not blacks so much as very dark blues. Stars peeking out, the stoic trees reaching their half-dead branches like lace against the sky. And yes—there are things that die in the winter. But there is more to the story than that.

I am thirty-one now, and the gray hairs are multiplying, springing out of the part in my hair at an alarming rate. Eventually I'll think about getting highlights, maybe.

But not tonight.

Tonight I'm thinking about the slivered moon, the amazing brightness of a simple reflection, the complex beauty of light. Tonight I'm thinking about the road trip—the one I'm on now. The one I've been on all this time.

Turn on the ignition. Begin your journey, and do not skip ahead.

I lie on the deck another moment. I stand up, take a long, grateful breath of the wintering air of my home state. Then I slide through the patio door, turn out the kitchen lights, and climb the stairs to my bedroom, where my husband is waiting for me in bed.

Acknowledgments

To the families, friends, readers, and kindred strangers who hosted us on our Epic Winter Road Trip—ten thousand *thank-yous* for your hospitality and for letting me share the ways your stories intersected for a brief window one February with mine.

In particular, I'd like to thank Steve, Dawn, Hope, and Esben Sandoval for being so honest about your family's struggle with chronic pain and for the redemptive, beautiful ways you are living out your lives in the dark. (Follow the Sandovals' journey and support them at www.facebook.com/StephenFights.)

To my Minnesota people, who have offered rest breaks and McDonald's french fries and love as I journeyed through the writing of this book—thank you. Specifically, I'd like to thank Judy Hougen and Rachel Riebe for reading long drafts in very short windows of time and for giving me thoughtful, careful edits, encouragement, and grace. I'd also like to thank Kenna Bjerstedt for being My Person; and the Sojourn women for teaching me what community looks like.

To the fine folks at The Bean in Andover—thanks for keeping me in coffee, wine, and sympathy while I wrote this book. Every writer needs a *place*. You're mine.

To my editorial team at Convergent—thanks for taking a chance on a weird road trip book where no murders are committed and nothing terrible happens. To my wonderful agent, Rachelle, thanks for talking me down.

To Kim and Alissa—the first time the darkness hit, you said, "Let's take a road trip to Memphis," and it changed everything. All of the most important things I know about healing, being honest, and moving forward I learned from you. Thank you.

To my parents, siblings, and in-laws—your love makes me brave.

To Dane and Liam—thanks for letting me tote you across the country for two weeks. You are teaching your mama not to be afraid of the dark.

To Andrew—thank you for letting me run away. Thank you for being the place I always want to come home to. I love you.